THE LAST OF THE HANDMADE DAMS
The Story of the Ashokan Reservoir

Bob Steuding

Professor of English and Philosophy
Ulster County Community College
Stone Ridge, New York

PURPLE MOUNTAIN PRESS, LTD.
Fleischmanns, New York

First published by Purple Mountain Press, Ltd. 1985
Second printing, 1986
Third printing, 1986

REVISED EDITION, 1989

Second printing, 1991

For information address the publisher:
Purple Mountain Press, Ltd.
Main Street, Fleischmanns, NY 12430

Library of Congress Cataloging-in-Publication Data

Steuding, Bob.
The last of the handmade dams : the story of the Ashokan Reservoir / Bob Steuding. -- Rev. ed.
p. cm.
Bibliography: p.
Includes index.
ISBN 0-935796-00-2
1. Ashokan Reservoir (N.Y.)--History. I. Title.
TD225.A76S74 1989
333.91'11'0974734--dc20 89-9381
CIP

Designed by Wray Rominger
Map by Janet Allison
Photo of the author by Martha Steuding

Printed in the USA

To my father Robert Steuding,
to Elwyn Davis,
and to Alf Evers
– master teachers and historians
each in his own way –
this book is dedicated
with gratitude and
admiration.

CONTENTS

Acknowledgments

The author gratefully acknowledges the assistance and munificence of numerous individuals. It is his hope that, if he neglects to name anyone through oversight, he will be forgiven. Among this long list of generous souls are Claudia Adsit, Joe Boack, Russell Boice, Herman Boyle, Frank and Nicholas Brown, Mrs. William Burger, Jim Burggraf, Ollie Burgher, Rosalie Burgher and the staff of the Olive Free Library, E. Wilson Burroughs, Patricia Carroll and the staff of the Ulster County Community College Library, Mr. and Mrs. Caruthers, Joe Cohen, Milton Combs, Herbert Cutler, Mrs. Kenneth Davenport, William Davenport, Carol and Charles Davis, Elwyn Davis, Mrs. Ferris Davis, Bob East, Harry Elder, Mrs. Cloyd Elias, Alf Evers, Charlie Field, Alfred Fox, William Golden, Ethel Gray, Kathryn Heavey, Bob Haines, Janet Harrington, Herbert Haufrecht, Irving Hesley, Joe Hudela, Maurice Hungiville, Mr. and Mrs. Hugh Kelly, Ester Kelsey, Linda and Bruce Kelso, John Kemble, Jennie Kerr, Josephine Lee, Aunt Fue Le Fevre, Michael Le Fevre, Edward Leverett, "Mac" Mac Creery, Thomas MacNamara, Harlowe McClain, Dan McCormack, Al Marks, S. James Matthews, Hope Miller, Tom Miner, Ed Ocker, Dennis O'Keefe, Mrs. Ernest Palen, Kent Reeves, Jay Rifenbary, Hobart Rowe, Barry Samuels, Whitty Sanford, Robert Schaedle, Edward Schwall, Mr. and Mrs. Herbert Shultz, Ethel Shurter, Linda and Robert Sleight, Agnes Scott Smith, Frederic Snyder, Willard Squier, Dale Stein, Nelly Strickland, Bill Swan, Ed Thiel, Arline Tisch, John Tisch, Kevin Umhey, Mrs. Sam Ware, Mabel Weidner, Herb Wells, Arthur Wicks, James Winston, Jr., Randolph Winston, Francis Wolven, and Eleanor Wuest.

In addition to the libraries cited above, my research was also conducted with the help of the following institutions: the Adjutant General's Office and the State Library in Albany, the New York State Historical Association Library at Cooperstown, the library of the New-York Historical Society and the New York Public Library in New York, the Franklin D. Roosevelt Library in Hyde Park, the Adriance Public Library and the Vassar College Library in Poughkeepsie, the library at the State University of New York at New Paltz, the Kingston Area Library and other area libraries in Woodstock, Hurley, West Hurley, Phoenicia, and Saugerties, the Greene County Historical Society Library at Coxsackie, the library in the New York City Board of Water Supply laboratory at Ashokan Station, and the Senate House Library in Kingston. I thank the efficient and competent staffs of these important repositories of historical information.

A part of the research for this book was completed while on sabbatical from Ulster County Community College and was funded, in part, by a grant-in-aid from the Research Foundation of the State University of New York. I heartily thank both institutions, as I do the Catskill Center for Conservation and Development for permission to reprint my article "Captured Spirits" from their publication.

And finally, I would like to tender a special thanks to my superb typist Monica Freer, a local historian in her own right; to Patty Kelly for keyboarding the revised edition; to Janet Allison for drafting the fold-out map; to Richard Katims, teacher, poet, and comrade; and to my family, my wife Martha and son Miles, who encouraged and supported me during those long hours in the field and at the desk.

Preface to the Revised Edition

The Ashokan Reservoir covers nearly 13 square miles of land. At the turn of the century, when the City came to the Catskills in search of pure water, it burned and leveled villages and razed homesteads and farms. Thousands of bodies were exhumed, a greater number, in fact, than the living who were dispossessed. Old photographs depict a township in ruin, only the stonewalls, which had once separated properties, remain. “It was like the end of the world,” remembers a soft-spoken, white-haired gentleman, who had worked as a teamster during the construction.

When I was a boy growing up near the reservoir in Hurley, I was mysteriously affected by this man-made body of water. I would ride my bicycle up to the reservoir and sit staring out across Ashokan toward the mountains in the west. My wife Martha and I came here many times before our marriage, discussing what we would do with our lives, planning how we would live. Upon our return to the Catskills, after college, marriage, and extensive travels abroad, we purchased an old stone house near the Ashokan Dam. I even prepared the first classes I taught at Ulster County Community College two decades ago in a warm, bright fall on the rock ledges at its shore. My son Miles caught his first fish in the reservoir. Clearly, the Ashokan has meant a great deal to me.

As a young boy with the world before me, however, I was unaware that another young person, with dreams and ambitions perhaps like my own, had lost his life in the stone crusher at the dam site, or that black muleteers from Virginia had driven their big wagons from the sandpits, cracking their long whips and standing up, or that many local farmers had sold their ancestral land to the City for a song. Sitting on the riprapping of the dam, I could not have heard the creaking cables once suspended from the great derricks which had towered overhead long years ago. Ashokan has long been silent.

Even today, when I speak to groups of schoolchildren about the reservoir, I am frequently asked whether houses still exist down below, as if Ashokan were some sort of mountain Atlantis buried beneath the sea. During the recent drought, a newspaper from downstate reported that observers had seen a church steeple rising from the ebbing waters. And so the mystery of Ashokan and its history persists to this day.

It is not surprising, then, that when *The Last of the Handmade Dams* was published by Wray and Loni Rominger of Purple Mountain Press, and the book reached the bookstores in a bitterly cold week before Christmas three years ago, it was received with interest. The extent of that response, however, I could not have anticipated. For in a few weeks, the book sold out, was reprinted, and then reprinted again. It was a very exciting time for us. To date, the demand remains constant. And the enthusiasm with which the book is still received cheers me, offering encouragement during the long and arduous process of writing my next book, "Rondout: the Story of a Hudson River Port."

The warm letters I have received, the delightful telephone calls, the invitations to speak, all these communications have confirmed in me the belief that people are not oblivious to their history, nor unconcerned about the places in which they live. Although the pace and shape of life has changed greatly since the dawning days of this century, and it would seem that television, superhighways, and the proliferation of shopping malls have irrevocably altered the pattern of small town rural life. I would like to think that this interest in local history offers some hope for the future. For through a greater understanding of the history of the place in which one lives, it could be suggested, one may become more profoundly respectful of that place and the good life that can be lived there. If this book in any way furthers such an awareness, I shall be deeply gratified.

B.S.
Olivebridge, New York
January, 1989

PROLOGUE

A WEDGE OF GEESE arrows past overhead, beating out of sight beyond the humpbacked bulk of South Mountain. Sunlight slants in from the southwest, suffusing the large porch with a warm glow. The leaves of the maples are golden. It is the end of a soft fall day in the Catskill Mountains.

We sit in wicker chairs facing the blue expanse of the Ashokan Reservoir. "You have to sort of prompt me a bit," says the old man whose name is Elwyn. "They get in the back of my mind, and they just have to rise gradually to the surface." Elwyn's speech is slow; he pauses ever so slightly, as he reaches the last phrase, lingering on the significant word "gradually," cherishing it and his long life in that brief pause. Then softly, with declining intonation, he relinquishes the rest of the phrase. He smiles, more to himself than to me.

I am awkward with this folklore taping. I had called it that name when I borrowed the recorder. Now I am less sure of myself. The batteries of the recorder are dead, I realize, and I have brought no extension cord with me. I do not want to loose a single word of what this old man is saying, and I have already lost many. Embarrassed, I ask him if he has a cord, and he rises slowly, his chair creaking, and goes into the house. The door slams and I hear him rummaging around inside. He returns with an electrical relic and begins to unscrew the light bulb which dangles precariously above my head. "This what you want?" he asks tauntingly, holding up the frayed wire. I shall remember this tone of voice and hear it so often again in the coming years. He inserts a screw socket and then plugs in the cord. I make the connection; the recorder whirs and the tape slithers from one side of the cassette to the other making a swishing sound. Elwyn settles back into his chair. He looks at me. It is a slow, direct, careful stare. "Just tell me what you want to know," he says after a time. Then, our conversation runs in bumps and starts. I find that at first I am hesitant to probe this man's knarled past. One which I realize he distinctly enjoys recollecting and relating. Soon Elwyn is deep in remembrance. Occasionally, he meditatively sips port wine from a little jelly jar, smacking his lips. His old eyes, which I had thought were dull at first, begin to shine. I find myself back at the end of the nineteenth century, walking the tracks of the U & D Railroad with a fat little farm boy. We are going to school in old West Shokan.

"I was never much of a scholar," relates Elwyn. "I flunked the exam for my high school diploma." But I marvel at his grasp of history and local human events. He shoots out his threads of life and lore, and I am slowly, yet inexorably, caught up in the web of his rememberings. It is a process he will repeat over the three years I shall know him, one which will not end with his final illness and death. I will say goodbye to Elwyn at his grave in the same cemetery which embraced the dead exhumed from the floor of the Ashokan. But it is a friendship, one-sided at times, which I still must admit exists, unbroken by the seeming finality of the grave. In my mind, Elwyn and his world of so long ago, the world of wagons and sawmills, bear hunting and rattlesnakes, tanneries and bluestone quarries, still exist.

The story of this relationship deals with what anthropologists call "rites of passage," that is, ritualized observances which punctuate the story we call life and give it shape and significance. Our relationship always had this sense of importance. There was always something occurring between Elwyn and me which transcended mere conversation. Something more was being passed on than information. It was like the sounds a dog, but not a man, can hear. I realized quite early during the course of our talks that the construction of the Ashokan Reservoir was merely the occasion, the excuse even, for those discussions. Elwyn was the embodiment of the past I wanted to know and understand, to contact, as if at a seance in which the dead who had lived before me could speak through him again. I believe Elwyn knew this also. As I was attempting to learn and to grow in my knowledge of these mountains, Elwyn was in the process of facing his death and trying to preserve the shape of his life and the country as he knew it. Our orientations were different, but we were heading in the same direction.

In the three years of our association, Elwyn was to pass on to me a great deal of what he had seen and felt. And this transference was to become for me a burden as well as a responsibility. In fact, there came a point when I literally began to see the old towns and houses, long gone, as I drove across the dam and looked to the west. Doubtless, this was some sort of superimposition on my mind of the many photographs I had seen of the valley before its inundation. I know this. But at this time it spooked me. I began to realize that I was slipping back into the misty world of Elwyn's past. Our conversations were not ending when I turned off the tape recorder and left the white frame house on the hill. Slipped from my moorings, I was floating out into the deep, murky sea of the past. I stopped our conversations for a time, I remember.

These talks were a meeting of two worlds. In a sense, while we talked, both Elwyn and I did not exist. Only what had happened had any substance, any corporeal reality. Now that our dialogue has ceased and I have returned from a long journey of another sort, I can see more clearly what I have learned. And the realization of what Elwyn has passed on to me comes in a hot rush. It is not only the lore of an era that has floated into the mists of time like a hawk into the fog-shrouded tops of a Catskill peak. It is something more concrete, more permanent. It is that knowledge which Elwyn himself groped toward in those last three years of his life. It is not only history, or the sense and shape of the past, which Elwyn's stories unfolded to me. What I learned was written on his face, as well as spoken by his childlike mouth. It was what all of us come to know about life. As Ernest Hemingway has written, "I have searched all my life for truth. Now I know that it is all true." It is that past, present, and future are one. In the strict sense of the term, there is no history. There just is.

In the end I think I must admit that I failed Elwyn. It was inevitable, I know. What Elwyn wanted was to stay alive, to be young again, to be caught at the lip of the high water falls he was rushing towards. No one can do this, of course, and I think that if this knowledge ever surfaced to his consciousness during those last years, he would have admitted that what I write is true. Elwyn clung to me and to the other searchers who went to him in order to learn the old ways. He received full-measure for his time. He gained a greater sense of reality for himself through this connection with us. Yet, I cannot help experiencing that mixed feeling of righteousness and guilt, even now, as I write this. We cling with great tenacity to those whom we feel possess life in seemingly greater quantity. It would seem now, that it was not simply a matter of me being unable to let Elwyn go into his grave, although I was one of the few who cried when his coffin was lowered into the rocky mountain earth. Without ever saying so, Elwyn had made it clear that what he passed on to me was not mine to keep. I was to continue the song, teach it to others. And so, I write this.

Chapter 1

INTRODUCTION

THE INDIANS first called it Ashokan. It had no name before they came, a short, slender, olive-skinned people. "Place of many fishes," is one translation of the name they gave this locale of rapidly flowing clear water at the base of the first ramparts of the mountains the Dutch settlers would in turn call the Catskills, the wild cat mountains, or the Blue Mountains, looking off with awe and fear into the western distances. As the waters receded from this area some 300 million years ago, and the land rose and fell over the eons of unfathomable time, Ashokan became swampy, the climate warm and humid. Shockingly large plants and animals lived here. The silence was incredible. After a time, which no human being experienced, the weather gradually became colder, and the climate changed. Then, the ice came. It pushed and groaned inexorably downward from the North like some gigantic white beast, grinding and gouging the land and shearing off all vegetation in its path. Finally, the ice retreated, then came again, retreated and returned many times. Once Ashokan became a vast glacial lake, when the space between what would later be called High Point and Overlook Mountains was plugged by glacial debris. What remained as this most recent ice sheet slowly, grudgingly departed, were the rocks and boulders of glacial morraine, the lakes and pot-holes, and the notches in the mountains where the rushing, melting waters had cut through the softer sandstone shales on their route to the river valley below, and ultimately to the sea.

The Indians first followed these swollen streams and climbed through the glacial cuts into the area some 6,000 to 8,000 years before the birth of Christ. Before the grandeur of Greece and the glory of Rome, the Esopus Indians had hunted here and moved through this territory on their journeys to visit fellow Delaware, or Leni Lenape, as they called themselves. They were an Algonkian-speaking people, unrelated to the more famous and warlike Iroquois to the north and west. The *Walam Olum*, a bark manuscript of sorts, relates the story of their ancient migration from the coast to this mountainous locale. A trapper named Bartlet is said to have been the first white man to enter this area. Following the Esopus Creek up from its mouth at the Hudson River, he built a post in Ashokan and traded with the aboriginals. But, of course, nothing of his post remains to this day. And no one knows what he looked like, or even how exactly to spell his name. By the time, much later, when the descendants of the first Dutch farmers who had settled in the valley of the Hudson were granted land up in Ashokan by the British representative, Lord Cornbury in 1704—men with names such as Brodhead, Middagh, Jansen, and Bogart—the Indians had seen the impact of the white man's ways on their pattern of living and on the land. Many had moved from the area after the Indian Wars of the 1660s. During these wars, they had burned Kingston twice and killed many of these lowland farmers; but countless others had come to replace them. A number of forts would be built in the Catskills by the patriots during the Revolution in order to prevent the Indians from assisting the British. One was constructed at Ashokan along the Esopus at the head of a hollow heading south. But none of these forts saw action. Not a shot was fired. And few Indians were seen in Ashokan after this time. Only the names and legends remain. Tongore, Moonhaw, Peekamoose, Shandaken, Ashokan are local place names which inadequately chronicle the Indian past here.

Primitive roads were cut through this virgin wilderness during the eighteenth century. Then, with the pressure of increasing settlement from New England and from Delaware County after the Revolution, the old Indian trails up the streams and through the glacial cuts were deepened and widened. In the early nineteenth century, hemlock planks from the tanneries and sawmills, which were springing up like mushrooms on the forest floor, covered the old trails, and the Indians who first pioneered them after the retreating glacial sheet were quickly forgotten. A man could hardly think with the deep, ear-splitting rumbling of the huge wagons carrying the stinking hides of South America up from the sloops on the Hudson to the tanneries in the mountains. Others followed these noisy corduroy roads up into Ashokan, the air filled with the swirling red dust of the hemlock bark which was crushed into big vats to tan the hides. These pioneers came to peel bark, to haul logs, to cook and wash dishes and clothing. They were a hardy lot. They lived up in the damp, green mountains in log shanties, and fought the cold and snow in winter and the flies and mosquitoes in summer. Most of these workers, like birds in the fall, left when the bark disappeared about the time of the Civil War. But others obtained land and remained. These first settlers became farmers, and they laid the plough to the rocky but fertile soil which was exposed by the passing of the great hemlock forests. It was said that before the bark peelers had cut down the forest, a man could hardly see his hand in front of his face, even at noonday. These later settlers who came with the tanneries inhabited even the highest hollows in the mountains. They planted hay, oats, rye, corn, potatoes and other foodstuffs for the consumption of man and beast. For nearly a century they shaped a way of life out of these mountains and off this land once carved by glacier and crossed by Indian braves.

Soon, a turnpike was built, and then, the railroad. With the road and the train came the opportunity to sell farm and forest products to more distant markets, and thus the economy of the region was altered. Huge slabs of sandstone, or "bluestone," were cut from quarries high on Catskill mountainsides for the sidewalks of New York City. Dragged down the mountains by oxen, the stone was taken by wagon to the great stone docks at Wilbur near Kingston on the Rondout Creek. Charcoal was also manufactured up in a side hollow of the Moonhaw at the foot of Balsam Cap Mountain in large kilns. The grimy men, called "colliers," who tended these kilns during the long dark vigil of three nights, were feared by one and all. Maltby, who owned the kilns, gave the hollow its present name. And also, with the railroads came droves of summer tourists who yearned to escape the crowding, heat, and disease of the city. The local response to this temporary population explosion was the rapid growth of the boarding house industry. After the 1870s it seemed, everyone who possessed a spare bed took in someone during the summer.

This brief bonanza, however, was to come to an abrupt end. For at the turn of the century, the City of New York came to Ashokan. And unlike the seasonal tourist, it came to stay, constructing a great dam on the Esopus Creek at Olive Bridge, creating a giant reservoir, and thus inundating the valley inhabited by the ancestors of the early settlers. This multimillion dollar project, in a few short years, was to change literally the shape of this land and to alter irrevocably its older, established way of life. Never again would Ashokan rest in sleepy, rural peace. The aggressive march of urban growth, with its insatiable thirst for pure, fresh water, had reached the Catskill Mountains. And Ashokan, caught squarely in its path, would never be the same.

Chapter 2

PREPARATIONS

WHEN WATER from the new Croton Aqueduct entered the Central Park Reservoir in 1890, it seemed as if New York City's chronic water problems were over. And yet, in less than ten years, the consumption had increased so rapidly, jumping from 102 million to 170 million gallons per day, that it had threatened to overtake the supply.[1] By 1900, New York City was consuming approximately 500 million gallons of water a day. Such a quantity of water, if released down Fifth Avenue, would have risen to the height of a man's waist, if collected, would have weighed approximately eight times that of the city's entire population. Due to the influx of unprecedented numbers of immigrants and its inability to prevent waste and to ration water supplies, the City found itself, once again, in a state of "water famine," as it was then called. This was a familiar situation, however. For most of its history, New York had used more water than could be supplied. As early as 1775, an Irish-born civil engineer by the name of Christopher Colles had proposed to erect a reservoir for the city and convey water through the streets in wooden pipes made of pine. Also, since the digging of the first well in 1677 by the Dutch at Bowling Green, wastes had drained into open gutters and into the soil, thus ultimately finding their way into the water system and hopelessly contaminating it. These wretched public health conditions affected staggering mortality rates. In an effort to address this problem, in the early years of the Republic, the Manhattan Company was incorporated by the City. This private corporation, later much criticized, as were all the private companies involved in the acquisition and distribution of water, was headed by the notorious Aaron Burr, who in 1800 lost the Presidency to Thomas Jefferson in a deadlocked election, and four years later killed his bitter enemy Alexander Hamilton in a duel. The Manhattan Company, which was given the exclusive right to provide the City with water, sunk a well near the Collect, built a reservoir on Chambers Street of over 1/2 million gallon capacity, and supplied water through wooden mains to 400 families. By 1830, however, pure water was still only available to 1/3 of the population, and so the first public waterworks were constructed, a tank being supplied by a well at 13th Street and filled by steam engine. This supply proved completely inadequate, however. Thus, in 1832, Colonel DeWitt Clinton, a civil engineer, was engaged to study the problem. His report proposed that a low dam, north of the City, be built on the Croton River, and that its waters be diverted by aqueduct to the City. Subsequently, and after much controversy and compromise, the Croton Dam was constructed, the work accomplished between 1837 and 1842. Between 1857 and 1862 a new Central Park Reservoir was also built. And yet, in 1869, 1876, 1880, and 1881, New York suffered still from drought and consequent water shortage. Even the new Croton Reservoir became insufficient. And so, it appeared that the City would have to search beyond the Croton watershed for a new source of supply.

The initial move in this direction, interestingly, occurred not in Manhattan, but across the East River in Brooklyn. On November 2, 1896, the Manufacturers' Association of Brooklyn appointed a special committee, headed by Charles N. Chadwick, to investigate the problem. Chadwick and his committee, after careful study, recommended on March 15, 1897, that west of the Hudson River be considered as a possible source of water for Brooklyn. Predicting such an eventuality, and having been influenced by an article by R. D. A. Parrott published in *Scientific American* (September 4, 1886), which had first suggested the Esopus Creek in the Catskill Mountains of Ulster County as a source of water for New York City, another private company, called the Ramapo Water Company, began quietly to acquire options on water rights throughout New Jersey, Connecticut, and upstate New York. The company, created by a coalition of powerful politicians from both parties, easily secured from the state legislature powers wider than those of municipalities to obtain these water rights.[2] By simply filing plans with the local county clerk, the company could acquire both reservoir rights and routes for aqueducts. Any objecting property owner was required to file a protest within 15 days and guarantee the expenses of an inquiry. In the case of aqueducts, the property owner was also expected to provide an alternate route, which in the opinion of a qualified engineer, would be more favorable to the company. When New York City, after the consolidation of its separate municipalities in 1899 created a giant metropolis of over 3 million people, finally faced the problem of obtaining an additional water supply, it found its efforts hampered by the Ramapo Water Company, which had, by this time, tied up all available sources. That August the company offered to supply the City with 200 million gallons of water per day at a cost of $70 per million gallons.[3] In addition, the contract they proposed was to remain in force for 40 years, the ultimate expenditure by the City amounting to over $200 million dollars.[4] Having been prepared in secret, the contract was sprung on the Board of Public Improvements by Water Commissioner William Dalton, with the asssurance that the majority of the Board would accept it. However, one Commissioner named Shea and the Comptroller, Bird S. Coler, opposed the contract. Although voted down by the rest of the members of the Commission, Coler was able to obtain a two week delay in which to consider the proposition. This was sufficient time for his needs, however; for by the next day, the public had learned of the Ramapo scheme, and a tumultuous outcry of indignation had arisen, creating a great sensation, and delaying the acceptance of the contract. Immediately after obtaining the delay, Comptroller Coler, who had alerted the press, also initiated a thorough study by a group of disinterested engineers headed by John R. Freeman. Freeman's report submitted on March 23, 1900 presented the facts of the matter to Comptroller Coler, regarding the viability of the existing water systems, the use and the waste of water, and the need for additional water supplies, at least 300 million gallons per day more than the Ramapo Company had offered. Significantly, the report soundly condemned the proposed Ramapo contract on many grounds, and recommended that the City develop its own water system.[5] Other private and civic organizations, among them the Merchants' Association, also commissioned independent investigations which reached findings and made recommendations similar to those of the Freeman study. The Ramapo water would cost twice the rate of that obtained from the Croton supply, and for less than the sum which the City would be contracting for, it could construct its own entirely new system, and not find itself in the same position in 40 years when the contract ran out. Although Water Commissioner Dalton continued to defend the contract and state that he felt it was unnecessary to investigate the Ramapo project, since he had personally visited the sites of the proposed reservoirs and found them to be sufficient, at the end of the two week delay, the project was dead and the contract unsigned. Ultimately, in March of 1901, Governor Roosevelt, at the urging of Coler and William Randolph Hearst of the *New York Journal*, secured the repeal of the Ramapo Company charter, and no one dared to mention the subject again. (However, for 15 years, the company sought unsuccessfully in the courts for damages). Thus, through the watchful stewardship of Comptroller Coler, and the consequent public and governmental response, the Ramapo scheme was exposed, and the City gained the right to build and operate a publicly-owned water system.

No progress was made for some time in undertaking this project, however, until the new mayor, Seth Low, took office. The previous administration, which had been identified with the Ramapo scheme, had fallen into disfavor, and consequently, little had been done. The first positive steps were taken by Mayor Low in December of 1902, when he appointed William H. Burr, Rudolph Hering, and John R. Freeman to act as members of a Commission on Additional Water Supply. Low directed them to undertake an exhaustive investigation of the matters of waste, consumption, and supply. A large staff was assembled, and in the research, which took nearly a full year, no stone was left unturned. Their voluminous report, submitted to the new Water Commissioner Robert Grives and to Mayor

Low on November 30, 1903, contained in detail definitive plans for improving existing waterworks, but also for developing additional water supplies from sources both east and west of the Hudson River, most notably, from the Esopus, Rondout, Schoharie, and Catskill watersheds in the Catskill Mountains.[6] It proposed to bring these combined Catskill waters, gathered together with those east of the Hudson, by aqueduct to the City. The first stage in this project would be accomplished by constructing a dam higher than that proposed by the Ramapo Company at Olive Bridge on the Esopus Creek. Dutchess and Rockland Counties, however, were alarmed by this prospect, fearing the loss of their own water rights. Adamantly against the construction of a New York City water system in their domain, they united and initiated in 1904 legislation prohibiting the City from taking land east of the Hudson. In response, the City considered attempting to repeal this legislation, but did not, choosing the seemingly easier course of finding another source. In turn, the interstate waters of Ten Mile River, which could be developed in less time at lower cost, were considered and then rejected, due to legal objections which were raised. The nearest large body of water, the Hudson, was found to be unsuitable, because of its high level of pollution, which would require expensive filtration. Even the Adirondack Mountains and the Great Lakes were considered, but the enormous expense of utilizing these sources precluded their development. Thus, there seemed no place else to look, as the Ramapo Company had known all along, other than Ulster County and the Catskill Mountains. It was only a matter of time before the Catskill Water System was proposed.

In this regard, and quite importantly, an amendment to the State Constitution was ratified on November 8, 1904, which helped to increase the possibility of the dream of a city water system becoming a reality. That amendment removed capital expenditures for waterworks from the municipal debt limit, thus making it possible for the City to finance such a large undertaking. And so, the following year, with the population over 4 million and increasing at an alarming rate of 115,000 a year, the City appealed to the legislature. As a result, the McClellan bill was introduced, subsequently passed by a 2/3s majority, and signed into law by Governor Higgins on June 3, 1905. This law, heralded as a model of non-partisanship and public-spiritedness, stands in sharp contrast to the shady dealings of the Ramapo Company. With that scandal in mind, no doubt, and in an effort to safeguard and control the water resources of the state in the future, the legislature also passed a second bill creating a regulatory body called the Water Supply Commission. These two bills became Chapter 724 and Chapter 723 respectively of the Laws of 1905. Chapter 724 of the Laws of 1905 provided for ". . .an additional supply of pure and wholesome water for the City of New York; and for the acquisition of lands or interest therein and for the construction of the necessary reservoirs, dams, aqueducts, filters and other appurtenances for that purpose; and for the appointment of a commission with powers and duties necessary and proper to attain these objects."[7]

In less than a week after the passage of this law, Mayor George B. McClellan, who upon taking office in 1904 had evinced a strong interest in providing the City with a new supply of water, appointed as Board of Water Supply Commissioners J. Edward Simmons (who later resigned and was succeeded by John A. Bensel), Charles N. Chadwick, and Charles A. Show. The Corporation Counsel of the City was made the attorney and legal advisor of the Board, and the Comptroller of the City was authorized and directed to raise from the issuance of corporate stock of the City money to defray the Board's financial obligations.[8]

During the summer of 1905, one of the first acts of the Board was to appoint John R. Freeman, who had written the original report back in 1900, as Consulting Engineer to the Board. William H. Burr, author of the later and longer report of 1903, and Frederick P. Stearns also became consulting engineers on an advisory board. In addition, the Board appointed J. Waldo Smith as Chief Engineer. This simple appointment proved to be one of the most important and fortunate acts which the Board ever made. For Smith, who began his duties on August 1, 1905 at an annual salary of $15,000, was an extremely good choice. Photographs of J. Waldo Smith show a physically small man of erect carriage, with a strong, encouraging face, and large, intense eyes peering from behind round black eyeglasses. He had been born in Lincoln, Massachusetts on March 9, 1861, had attended Phillips Academy at Andover, and was an 1887 graduate of the Massachusetts Institute of Technology. At the age of 15, he had worked on the construction of a water supply for Lincoln, and had been named its Chief Engineer at 17. At 20 he had been employed in the engineering department of the Essex Company in Lawrence, Massachusetts, which operated the water power of the Merrimac River. During his summer vacations from M.I.T., Smith worked with the Holyoke Water Power Company, and after graduation, served from 1887 to 1890 as their assistant engineer. In 1890 Smith became the assistant engineer for the East Jersey Water Company and for the next 12 years was engaged in the construction and maintenance of a succession of water supply systems in northern New Jersey. In 1891, he was made the chief engineer of the company. In this capacity in 1901, he directed the design and construction of the Little Falls mechanical filtration plant, a pioneer of its kind. And the following year he supervised the completion of the new 7-1/2 million dollar water supply for Jersey City, which included the Boon Dam and a concrete aqueduct. In 1903 Smith assumed the duties of Chief Engineer of the Aqueduct Commission of New York City, taking charge of the construction of the New Croton Dam then underway, the largest masonry dam in the world at that time. Two years later, Smith became the Chief Engineer of the Board of Water Supply and, therefore, directed the construction of the Catskill Water Supply System. In 1918, Smith was awarded the John Fritz Medal, the highest honor in the engineering profession. He remained Chief Engineer of the Board for 17 years, and later became consulting engineer until his death of a heart attack at age 72 in 1933.

Equally important as was Smith's impressive talent as a civil engineer, was his ability to surround himself with able men as executives and consultants. He possessed the rare capacity to choose competent subordinates and to direct their work with skill and tact. In an era of engineers, he was what today might be called the consummate human engineer. All who worked for Smith became personally fond of him, and their *esprit de corps* and loyalty undoubtedly contributed to the success of the Catskill Water Project. One associate, Robert Ridgway, as engineer in charge of the Northern Aqueduct Department, wrote in his memoirs, "My association with J. Waldo Smith, for whom I developed a great admiration and affection, was inspiring."[9] And, "In my opinion, no one could have carried that great work to completion as ably and creditably as he did."[10] Smith's exceptional abilities and character were cited in his *Engineering News-Record* obituary: "Engineering judgement and intuition of (the) highest order were essential parts of his equipment. . . but to these he joined a great power over men—an almost magical ability to inspire loyalty and affection in all who worked for him, and at the same time to disarm and convince his opponents. Integrity, simplicity and justice, and a homely New England shrewdness combined to create his power. . . ."[11] At a dinner in his honor two years before his death, his example was revered in a poem written for the occasion, which stated, "None knew thee but to love thee/None named thee but to praise thee."

Chapter 3

HEARINGS

ON AUGUST 5, 1905 the State Water Commissioners, transported in the private railroad observation car, "Number 20," of Edward Coykendall, general manager of the Ulster and Delaware Railroad, made a visual survey of the Esopus Valley and then closeted themselves at the Grand Hotel at Highmount on the divide of the Hudson and Delaware Rivers. There they spent several days in conference discussing their strategy for successfully accomplishing the necessary legal steps for the conversion of the Esopus Valley into a reservoir. After this meeting, on August 7, the City Board of Water Supply passed a resolution directing the creation of a general plan for securing an additional supply of water from the Catskill Mountains district, instructing the Chief Engineer to submit plans and profiles. That report, when completed, was included in the master report submitted by the Board on October 9, 1905 to the Board of Estimate and Apportionment. It was accompanied by a large map and profiles presenting the complete plan for developing the Catskill watershed. The report was adopted by resolution by the Board of Estimate and Apportionment on October 27, 1905, filed with the State water authorities on November 3, and approved by them in May of the following year.

Such dispatch was, without a doubt, impressive. An engineering force and its support system had been mobilized and sent to work in the field in record time. However, it became the source of anger and resentment toward the City of New York. Impatient to go forward with the project, the Board of Water

Supply had sent drilling crews to the Esopus Creek at Tongore and Bishop's Falls on August 5, 1905 to obtain core borings in order to determine the depth of the bedrock, and thus to decide the location of the Ashokan Dam, which would impound a great reservoir of some 12.8 square miles. As water historian Charles Weidner writes, "With little regard for precedent or amenities, the Board began to make explorations and surveys preliminary to the construction of the Ashokan Reservoir months (about eight) before the State Water Commission approved the project."[12] As a result, residents of the Esopus Valley were unprepared for such a precipitate action, initiated by the impatience of the Board, which had acted before it had been given the right. This "invasion of private property"[13] was shocking. One old, gray-haired farmer remembered with ire until his death in 1976 how "City surveyors," as he called them, had cut down his mother's prize rose bushes without asking permission.[14] Other bitter memories of this sort of cavalier behavior toward locals, who with their lawyers were seen as country bumpkins and "Reubens of the first water," were not uncommon.[15] In an article printed in *The New York Times* the following year, the locale was dubbed "Aboriginal Ulster."[16] Certainly, Corporation Counsel John J. Delaney, it seemed to the residents of Ulster County, had expressed most explicitly the feelings of the Board and the City toward the inhabitants of the proposed reservoir site, when he stated flatly that "rural communities must be sacrificed for the needs of the great city."[17]

At this time the inhabitants of the Esopus Valley knew or cared little about the expansion of urban centers, or the burgeoning era of progess. But the progressive urbanite Theodore Roosevelt, who in 1904 had defeated for the Presidency Alton B. Parker, the rural gentlemen farmer from Ulster County, set the tone for the era, and from the White House commanded a vast and optimistic public works movement. Thus, in the long corridors of government, both in Washington and Albany, the voice of rural areas was only dimly heard; for so much louder were the cries of the big cities such as New York, the melting pot and entrance of immigrants, the first city to be electrified, the site of such engineering wonders as the Brooklyn Bridge, the Statue of Liberty, and Trinity Church. New York possessed the most important and vocal preachers, the most influential newspapers, and was a powerhouse of wealth and influence. At the turn of the century, New York was the fastest growing city in the most populous state. And it often decided the outcome in national elections. Along with this expansiveness of mood and the increasing political power of cities, technology and the engineer, the supreme technocrat, were idealized and utilized to achieve the ends of rapid and substantial growth. In this less cynical era, it was believed that there was nothing which applied science could not achieve or perfect, if man set his mind to the task and worked hard enough at it. Consequently, it was an era of dramatic social, economic, and political change, and those who could not adapt, or chose not to, suffered the consequences. Thus, country folk found themselves subject to the growing pressures of the nearby urban center, unsympathetic to the slower more plodding rhythms of an earlier agrarian pastoral tradition. As a result, rural dwellers felt themselves without adequate representation. And they began to perceive that their situation, once so stable and secure, was out of their control, the old pattern broken.

It was in this frame of mind of mixed anger, resentment, and fear that the residents of Ulster, and especially of the Esopus Valley, faced the coming of New York City, and awaited the hearings which would determine their fate, one which many believed had already been set. On November 27, 1905, upon receiving the city's application for the construction of a water system in the Catskills, the State Water Commission served public notice, as required by law, that it would meet at the Ulster County Court House in Kingston, New York for the purpose of hearing all persons, municipal corporations, and other civil divisions of the state that might be affected by this application. Seven public hearings were held between November 27, 1905 and February 20, 1906—five in Kingston and two in New York City. During the first hearing, more than 500 spectators were present. The City was represented by Assistant Corporation Counsel George L. Sterling and Corporation Counsel Delaney, who was described in the Kingston *Daily Freeman* as "corpulent, soft-spoken. . .with incipient side whiskers, who looks like an Englishman. . .and deports himself like a royal duke. . . ."[18] Called as witnesses for the City were Chief Engineer Smith and Consulting Engineers Burr, Stearns, and Freeman, a formidable group of experts. The City's application, nonetheless, was vigorously opposed. State Senator Linson of Kingston moved to dismiss the entire proceedings on the grounds that the City had not complied with the law in creating state and municipal water commissions. His motion was overruled. Then followed the objections filed by the City of Kingston, a number of townships in Ulster, Greene, and Schoharie counties, the City of Yonkers, the village of Peekskill, and dozens of other private and corporate business concerns and public utility companies. In all, 126 objections were made. Among the local attorneys, or "mountain lawyers," as they were called by the New York press, who presented these objections, was A. T. Clearwater.[19] Among others, Clearwater represented the Ulster and Delaware Railroad, the Board of Trade, the Chamber of Commerce, and various local banks. In 1905, Clearwater was at the height of his powers and had developed a statewide reputation. Alphonso Clearwater was a small man, with short, fine hair, bright, proud eyes, and a closely-cropped, pointed beard. He had been born in 1848 at West Point of Dutch and French Huguenot ancestry, a fact of which he was inordinately proud. Clearwater had studied law with local notables, and after being admitted to the bar in 1871, subsequently had been elected District Attorney and later County Judge and Chairman of the dominant Republican Party. He was a popular afterdinner speaker, an historian, and a writer on various subjects, among them criminology. It was said that his political power and reputation were so great in his later life, that when Clearwater asked then Governor Alfred E. Smith to make appropriations for a new copper roof on a public building in Kingston, the Governor, it is reported, answered, "By all means, give it to him, before he asks for gold." Some thought Clearwater "a pompous ass" and an "imposter." But others whom he represented, and who saw him in action at the 1905 hearings, considered him "a mighty, mighty smart lawyer." In their eyes, he was a "powerful man" in the community, and he "had connections." "He could bark right out, if the occasion demanded."[20] And that is exactly what Clearwater did at the hearings. His first attack, eloquently and elaborately presented, was made against the constitutionality of the legislation which created the Water Board. Then, he asserted that the benefit to the City of the proposed project was both temporary and incommensurate with its cost. He also added, somewhat apocalyptically, that the dam would represent a perpetual menance to towns downstream. No engineering skill could successfully domesticate the unpredictable Esopus Creek, he said. During the second day of hearings, however, Clearwater made his most significant point. No fair and satisfactory provision had been established, he asserted, for the notification of property owners whose land would be seized, nor for the payment of them of direct and indirect damages. The only notice to be given was the publication of a list of names and numbers which corresponded to parcels of land cited on a map filed with the County Clerk. Clearwater pointed out that, technically, property could be taken ten days after the map was registered, in some cases, without the owner even knowing about it. In addition, he made clear, that the land was to be purchased at 1/2 its assessed valuation. In 1905, assessed valuations on upstate properties "were extremely low, seldom representing the real value."[21] A property with a sale value of $5,000 might be assessed for $500, and the owner dispossessed and forced to move at ten days notice and the payment of only $250.

In his cross-examination of the City's chief witness, J. Waldo Smith, A. T. Clearwater gave no quarter. Smith, however, stood firm, answering all of Clearwater's questions honestly and fully. A spectator remembers that Smith's "grasp of the subject, his ability to think clearly. . .and his coolness and fairness, impressed all who heard him. . . ."[22] Clearwater could not but respect Smith, even though they were adversaries in this instance. In 1931, two years before the death of both Smith and Clearwater, a subscription dinner was held for Chief Engineer Smith, on the occasion of his 70th birthday, at the Hotel Astor in New York, and Clearwater was invited. Although ill and unable to attend, Clearwater responded warmly to the committee regarding his old adversary, and his letter was read to those attending the dinner. He wrote, "My battery of austere doctors have forbidden indulgence in any further festivities." But Clearwater adds, "If I were sure that at the end of milleniums I would find you (Smith) to greet me, I would have taken the chance, but by that time you will be building dams of emeralds, rubies, and pearls, and I would not be permitted to cross-examine you as to the cost of construction."[23]

In addition to A. T. Clearwater, his client, Samuel Coykendall, president of the Ulster and Delaware Railroad and the owner of large tracts of bluestone quarry in the Town of Hurley, also spoke against the project. He agreed with Clearwater regarding the future inadequacy of the proposed system, suggested the Adirondacks as a preferable source of water, and pointed out that local tourism would be dealt a devastating blow, the many boarding-house keepers losing an estimated 1/2 million dollars in profits each year. In addition, he believed that inhabitants of Ashokan would be terrorized by the introduction of an "army of workers," which would make the area undesirable. He lamented the fact that the reservoir would submerge a vast amount of valuable property, interfere with the rights of municipalities, abolish markets and other business opportunities, deprive labor of fixed and regular employment, and arrest the economic development of the locality.[24]

Although Clearwater, Coykendall, and other respected citizens of Ulster County spoke against the proposed reservoir, on May 14, 1906, at the conclusion of these lengthy hearings, the State Water Commission decided in favor of New York City, as many disgruntled observers had predicted all along. Nonetheless, the hearings had not been a waste of time for the inhabitants of Ulster County; for one fundamental principle had been established. Although it was determined that the City's plan to construct a water system was "justified by public necessity," it was made clear, beyond a doubt, that the rights of all parties must be equitably protected.[25] In this regard, the Commission found that the McClellan Act required amendment, in order to afford greater protection to the owners of the properties and businesses within the area to be taken by the City of New York. To this end, the Commission sponsored, and the Legislature passed, Chapter 314 of the Laws of 1906. Chapter 314 defined the City's responsibility in respect to eviction of property owners, provided for police protection for communities in the area of construction, and made provisions for the payment of direct and indirect damages. Thus, it would appear that some of the many objections made during the hearings had been heard.

The local newspapers, however, were not satisfied, and they made veiled references to possible violent retaliation against New York. Some locals remembered, in this regard, hearing about the Anti-Rent War of the 1840s, when tenant farmers in the Catskills revolted against their absentee landlords. It *had* been suggested the previous month that a "People's Rights War" might be brewing.[26] But no violence had followed the Commission's decision, and the project, actually already begun by J. Waldo Smith and his staff, shifted into high gear long before the official ceremony was celebrated on June 20 of the following year, when Mayor George B. McClellan turned the first sod at Garrison, New York with a shovel inlaid with silver by Tiffany.

Chapter 4

BIDS

BETWEEN APRIL 1, 1906 and January 1, 1907 a complete topographic survey of the area to be flooded had been surveyed and mapped in 5-foot contours, a job which required the search of some 2,000 deeds. As a result of the core borings taken at Bishop's Falls, Tongore, and Atwood further south along the Esopus Creek, it was decided in August by Dr. Charles P. Berkey, an expert geologist working for the Board of Water Supply, that the main dam should be located a short distance downstream below Bishop's Falls. In the previous century, a blind miller had lived here, who it was said, could tell the color of a horse by touch. This was also the site of a beautiful covered bridge spanning the Esopus Creek, which had been built many years earlier. Berkey's explorations had revealed that this site at Bishop's Falls in Olive Bridge, in contrast to the other two locations, showed "favorable indication," the glacial drift overlying the rock being of a dense impervious nature extending down to bedrock over which there was no intervening porous layer.[27] If the dam could have been constructed at Tongore, the reservoir would have been considerably larger. But, because bedrock could not be found, this was not possible. And so, the location of the dam was determined.

By the end of 1906, careful surveys had also been made in connection with the relocation of highways and the Ulster and Delaware Railroad, and it had been decided to divide the reservoir into two basins by constructing an overflow weir at Brown's Station. Sufficient stone quarries and sand deposits had been discovered on the site of the construction. And 800 soil samples had been taken to determine if it would be necessary to remove the topsoil in the flooded portion of the reservoir. Below the site of the dam, a measuring weir had been constructed in order to obtain accurate statistics regarding the flow yield of the Esopus Creek. By early summer of 1907, all this work had needed to be completed, in addition to the construction of two cofferdams placed 400 feet apart and the installation between these dams of two 8-foot diameter pipes. This was necessary in order to expose the river bottom in preparation for the Board to open the building of the dam to bidding. For by law, the Board was required to undertake all construction by contract based on bids received after public advertisement. (Consequently, no large labor force was employed directly by the Board.) After receiving a number of sealed bids, Contract 3, the largest to be let, was awarded jointly to MacArthur Brothers Company of New York City and to Winston and Company of Katonah, New York on August 31, 1907. This contract was for the construction of the Ashokan Dam and dikes, and amounted to 5.5 miles of masonry and hardpacked earth structures. The main dam itself was to be 1,000 feet long, 190 feet wide at the base, and 23 feet at its crest. The earthen wings of the dam would be 4,650 feet long. This dam was to be constructed of cyclopean masonry (cement mixed with large blocks of local bluestone), and would have drainage and inspection galleries. It would impound over 12 square miles of water and create a reservoir with a 40 mile shoreline. In all, it would drain a total of 250 square miles, and contain when full, 128 billion gallons of fresh mountain water, enough it was thought, to float two flotillas of President Roosevelt's world famous naval ships.

This contract, however, was not awarded without controversy. Initially, J. Waldo Smith had estimated that the building of the dam and dikes, excluding the West Hurley dikes and the headworks, would cost $12,841,000 (the total cost of the entire Catskill Water System was approximately $162 million). Of the five sealed buds, which were publicly opened by the Board of Water Supply on August 6, 1907, the $12,669,750 bid of MacArthur Brothers Company and Winston and Company was only the second lowest. The lowest bid, at $10,315,350, was made by the John Pierce Company of New York City, the other three bids ranging around $14 million or over. Nonetheless, on the recommendation of Chief Engineer Smith, and with the approval of his consulting engineers, MacArthur and Winston were awarded the contract; for it was agreed, after consulting John Pierce, that his bid for excavation and embankment work had been too low. Actually, Pierce, who was inexperienced at bidding, had planned to subcontract this work, failing to include this added cost in his bid. Seizing upon this opportunity, however, the *New York World* and its editor, Joseph Pulitzer, once again attacked the project. Earlier, the paper had named it the "Esopus Folly."[28] Pulitzer's complaint, possibly a reaction to the financial panic of 1907, when J. P. Morgan supervised the pooling of the funds of New York City banks in an effort to prevent financial chaos, was that this seeming act of favoritism indicated unwise over-expenditure and the general mismanagement of public funds. Pulitzer, therefore, demanded an immediate investigation, and called for the removal of the Water Commissioners from office. Certainly, it was difficult to explain to an irate public that Pierce was inexperienced, and as was later discovered, incompetent. All the public noted was the lower amount of his bid. And so, an investigation was, in fact, undertaken, Mayor McClellan appointing Colonel Thomas W. Symons, a former military aide to President Roosevelt and a specialist in canal construction, H. P. Gillette, an associate editor of *Engineering News*, and Daniel J. Houer to assist in the work. In November, this investigating committee submitted its report. Possibly influenced by negative publicity and public opinion, it found the MacArthur and Winston bid "excessive" and the Pierce bid "fair," suggesting that it would net the company "a reasonble profit," provided the work be "economically and properly managed."[29] Quite shockingly, late that December, the Commissioners of Accounts also recommended in a report to the Mayor that the Commissioners of the Board of Water Supply be put on trial for malfeasance of office. In response, Mayor McClellan sought the advice of Corporation Counsel F. K. Pendleton. And finally, cooler minds prevailed; for Pendleton promptly reassured the troubled mayor that the Board of Water Supply had acted strictly within the spirit and the letter of the law in awarding the contract to the second lowest bidder. Pendleton pointed out that the Board was not bound by law to award contracts to the lowest, or even to any bidder, if it saw fit. It was only enjoined to select the bid which, in its judgment, would "secure the efficient performance of the work. . . ."[30] When this legal point was finally made known, the Board was vindicated, although its President, J. Edward Simmons, subsequently resigned on January 28, 1908. It is interesting to note, that not long after the dust of this needless controversy had settled, as if to prove the sagacity, good faith, and prescience of J. Waldo Smith and the Board, John Pierce and Company failed and went into the hands of the receivers.

Chapter 5

CONSTRUCTION

IN THE FALL OF 1907, Ashokan was a busy place. Gone was the normal peace and quiet of this upstate New York rural locale. Red and white flags dotted the site of the future dam and dikes at the Esopus gorge, and even the land at the old Bishop's Falls House was bisected by these fluttering markers. This venerable local landmark would be the first structure to be dismantled. For in the spring of the following year (May 5, 1908), it would be replaced by the tail-towers of the cableways at the dam. In September, MacArthur and Winston had begun operations, and by winter they had made amazing progress, breaking many previously held construction records. Much of the site for the dam and dikes had been cleared, and the erection of housing had been started for the many employees who were arriving from all parts of the country. Temporary offices were set up, as were a bakery and a commissary, stocked with familiar and unusual foodstuffs. The grade and the right of way were prepared, so that the railroad could begin to handle the copious materials and machinery, which were beginning to arrive from the Cross River Dam, which Winston and Company had nearly completed. This heavy equipment included standard and narrow guage locomotives, railroad cars, Bucyrus and Atlantic steam shovels, Monarch and Kelly-Springfield steamrollers, Atlantic and Ohio traction shovels, and dump wagons. To repair these behemoths, a machine shop was also being erected. Also, during these first months, the site of the head-towers of the cableways at the dam were drained, the foundation of the power plant started, and the blockyard graded. By the last week of November, work had even been started on reinforcing the cofferdams at the main dam site in preparation for the excavation down to bedrock.

This impressive accomplishment, completed during the first months of the scheduled 84-month project, was due in great measure to the work of James O. Winston, one of the major partners of MacArthur Brothers and Winston and Company, holders of Contract 3. As was Chief Engineer Smith, James Winston was a man equal to the job of constructing the huge Ashokan Dam, and it was he who firmly and ably oversaw the project. Back in 1892, Winston had bid too high on the proposed Croton Dam, and thus had lost the contract. But in 1905, his company had been awarded $1,246,211.60 to build the Cross River Dam, which it had completed successfully. Initially, Winston and his brother had subcontracted canal work in Chicago for MacArthur Brothers. But in 1907, they had gone into partnership with that company, in order to bid on Contract 3 at Ashokan. By this time Winston had obtained the experience and the financial backing to undertake this awesome job, only rivalled by a contemporary engineering project of greater magnitude and public appeal, the building of the Panama Canal.

A tall, handsome man, dynamic and commanding in personality, James Winston had been born in 1865 on the family estate, "Malvern," in Louisa County, Virginia. His father had been a colonel in the Confederate Army and his mother, the daughter of a physician and a respected member of Southern society. According to one of his sons, James O. Winston was "a man of tremendous ambition and great brain power."[31] Unfortunately, however, due to the widespread devastation affected by the Civil War and the Reconstruction period, the fortunes of the Winston family had declined, and this bright young man was unable to attend college as planned. James, in fact, had been taught by his mother to read and write, only attending elementary school for 6 years. With few prospects in Louisa County, and with limited education, James and brother Tom left the family farm and traveled to nearby Richmond. Here they entered the freight transfer business. This business failed, but in 1886 James was hired by a firm building a railroad along the Ohio River in Kentucky. As commissary clerk and timekeeper, he worked all day and studied engineering texts at night, being promoted to foreman by the following year. Winston was so anxious to succeed that, in order to prevent delay in the early morning blasting operations, he would keep dynamite warm and dry by taking it to bed with him. In later years, his wife would call Winston "a shooting star," and would add, when you hook on to one, there is nothing to do but hang on.[32] And so by 1892, when he and his brother formed their first contracting company, this aristocratic son of the South, who it was said had little interest in and aptitude for mechanics, and who was never certain whether to use his left or right hand, but whose obsession was getting things done, was well on his way toward enjoying the success and respect he so dearly sought. In subsequent years, the construction of tunnels, bridges, highways, railroads, electric lines, aqueducts, dams, and reservoirs followed, increasing the wealth, as well as the prestige of this commanding Southerner. By the time of his retirement in 1933, Winston had established business connections along the Atlantic seaboard from New England to the Carolinas, and had held contracts amounting to over 100 million dollars. Those who remember Winston say he rode "stately horses," and liked cockfights and Italian automobiles. At the project in Ashokan, he rode in a chauffeured limosine costing $13,000, and constantly smoked big cigars. It was also rumored that he appreciated good liquor, as well as beautiful women, but this is unconfirmed. During the construction of the Ashokan Dam, Winston and his family lived in Kingston, and it is said that the Ulster and Delaware Railroad was, at times, held for him, when he took the train up to the work site in the morning.[33] With a courtly disposition and an iron will, Winston was, indeed, a man who knew what power was and how to use it. And this is exactly what he did in commanding the construction of the Ashokan Dam, the largest in the world at the time, appropriately called "the last of the handmade dams."[34]

Certainly, Winston had no difficulty in dealing with a brief and aborted labor strike, which occurred during the first full year of construction. It was April 29, 1908, and the work had progressed well. The camp then housed approximately 3,000 men, women and children. And the work of excavation at the dam site had begin. The main plant, which had been moved from Katonah, New York and reconstructed at Olivebridge in stages, was nearly completed. It consisted of four Lidgerwood traveling cableways having a clear span of 1,530 feet and a lifting capacity of 15 tons each. Tracks placed 150 feet above the bed of the creek enabled the 93 foot high towers of these derricks to be moved 600 feet up or down the stream. There were also cableway and hoisting engines, drills, channelers, and pumps, which were operated by compressed air furnished by a central power station located on the north bank of the Esopus Creek upstream from the dam. It was powered by four Ingersoll-Rand cross-compound air-compressors, with a total rated capacity of 12,000 cubic feet of air per minute, the equivalent of 1,600 horsepower, and five Babcock and Wilcox boilers rated at 265 horsepower each. The central power station also furnished air for work in the dikes and for the operation of the drills and engine at the Yale Quarry, situated about a mile from the dam site. This quarry, a source of bluestone, had been opened by Winston and Company, and had been connected to the work at the dam by a standard guage railroad, for which the company had erected an 85 foot high, 390 foot span steel trestle over the Esopus Creek some distance upstream of the dam site. Also at the plant were a blockyard and a cement storehouse with a capacity of 4,000 barrels. By October, 1911 1-1/2 million barrels of Alsen Portland cement from Catskill, New York had been used in the construction of the dam. Adjoining the storehouse was a crushing and mixing plant, utilizing No. 9 McCully and No. 6 Austin crushers. It was connected to the storehouse by a conveyor belt driven by steam from the central power plant. Truly, the magnitude of the project and the preparations for it were quite impressive.[35]

However, that spring day in 1908, the 100 workers at Brown's Station, who struck for a 5-cent increase in pay, demanding a raise from $1.20 to $1.25 per day, had their own concerns in mind. The first decade of this new century was an era of deepening class division, slackening social mobility, and thus of general labor unrest and agitation. The American

Federation of Labor had been founded in 1881, as had the more radical International Workers of the World in 1905, in response to these deteriorating social conditions. But the A. F. of L., at the time, tended to regard with contempt, and some thought even fear, the competition of unskilled workers. Thus, it did not attempt to organize them. In general, during these peak years of immigration, and on a public works project such as this, one of the last to draw extensively on unrestricted European labor, where 64% of the workforce was immigrants, there was little if any union interest or involvement.[36] Later in the year, however, but after this one day strike of day laborers had failed, James Winston having given each striker the choice of his job without a raise or a one-way railroad ticket out of town, the I. W. W. sent an organizer named Samuel A. Stodel to Ashokan to investigate conditions. It had been reported that workers were herded into "pens without ventilation," and that this housing was rented at an exorbitant rate, generating unfair profit to the contractor.[37] Actually, 86% of the laborers at Ashokan, who received from $1.20 to $1.60 per day, lived in dormitories provided by the company. There a single man could obtain a room and board for from $20 to $22.50 a month. This meant that the average unskilled worker spent about 65% of his earnings for food and lodging. Skilled workers, of course, received higher wages. For example, machinists, pipe fitters, pumpmen, and plumbers earned $2 or more per day; a stonemason almost $3; the powderman received $10.16 per week for his dangerous work. And the lowest paid individuals on the work force were the waterboys, who each took home the sum of $1 a day. The average monthly payroll at the high point of the work was between $150,000 and $200,000.[38]

It was also reported in the *New York World* that 20 days pay were withheld from each man by the contractor, and that these men were not paid in cash, but in brass checks which could only be redeemed at the company's store. In 11 days spent at the camp, Stodel later stated, he could not get a dollar bill changed. In response to these complaints lodged against MacArthur and Winston, then President Roosevelt, who had been involved in an earlier investigation of the project, sent James B. Reynolds to investigate. Reynolds made his investigation at about the same time that the Bureau of Factory Inspection, at the request of the contractors themselves, undertook its own special investigation to determine whether there had been compliance with all the provisions of the New York State Labor Law. The Bureau found that housing conditions were in compliance with the terms of the contract. However, they established that the "brass check" system, in operation at the time at the camp, although not used as a system of wage payment but as a form of credit for newly hired workers prior to their first pay, did, nevertheless, constitute a technical violation of the cash payment wages law. As a solution to this problem, the Bureau suggested that a cash advance of 1/2 the wages earned for a period of one month be given to each new worker. Regarding the price of goods and foodstuffs at the company commissary, another matter of complaint, the investigators found, that although neither exorbitant nor unreasonable, the prices were, in a number of cases, somewhat higher than those charged by local merchants. For example, butter which sold outside the camp for 20 cents a pound, cost 38 cents a pound in the commissary, and eggs, which sold for about 30 cents a dozen in the local stores, listed at 38 cents a dozen in the camp. No recommendations, however, were made in this regard.

The reporting of these incidents—the strike, the complaints, and the investigations—should not suggest that there was an unusual amount of worker discontent at Ashokan, or that MacArthur and Winston mistreated their workers, according to the standard of the times. The great majority of workers, in most respects, seem generally to have been satisfied, or at least accepted their lot and remained silent. The camp in which they lived was clean, functional, and well-maintained and operated. There were facilities and opportunities provided for recreation and relaxation, as well as the edification and betterment of these men. Nevertheless, it would seem that some of the complaints regarding wages and living costs were not entirely without foundation. Certainly, the somewhat restrictive circumstances and enforced conditions of the camp, created and maintained by the company and endorsed by the City of New York, made possible the potential exploitation of the unskilled, non-local and foreign workers. For these men, who toiled for a wage lower than that earned by local farm day laborers, were, for all practical purposes, forced to purchase their lodging, and most of their food, clothing, and other supplies from MacArthur and Winston, although living in the camp and trading in the company store were not compulsory. Of course, it was not unusual, at the time, for contractors to profit not only from the contract itself, but also from the maintenance of their workers.[39] Nonetheless, it can be said that progressive ideas regarding the relationship between labor and capital and their respective rights and responsibilities had not had an influence on public works projects of this type, conducted in the traditional manner where power rested firmly and exclusively in the hands of the contractor.

At the completion of these many investigations, the conditions, unfair or not, continued unabated, with only minor changes being made. Clearly, it was a time when few restrictions were placed upon employers, and there was little significant protection for the unorganized worker and his family. There was no compulsory workmen's compensation, no welfare for women and children, and no insurance against accident, illness, or old age. At about the time of Stodel's visit to the camp at Ashokan, the non-agricultural workforce in the United States amounted to some 30 million men and 8 million women. Between 33% and 50% of this population lived in poverty, working 50 to 70 hour weeks, often under unsafe and unsanitary conditions. Only one in ten of their children completed high school. And so, although the unskilled worker at Ashokan may seem by our present standards to have been exploited, in comparison to his contemporaries, he was treated rather well, being the first laborer on a public works project to work a 40-hour week and to regularly save a portion of his pay.

In this regard, it is interesting to note the difficulties experienced by peddlers, who attempted to sell and to deliver goods to workers in the camp; for these altercations indicate the control the contractor attempted to exercise over the camp and the conduct of business within it. Most of the peddlers, such as Sam Bluestein and Ike Gordon, who later settled in the area and established business, were Jewish. Due to the variety and the relative inexpensiveness of their wares, their arrival at camp was awaited with anticipation. However, in order to peddle on City property, these enterprising individuals were required to complete a lengthy application form, which relieved MacArthur and Winston and Company of liability, and bound the applicant to certain conditions. According to these conditions, under no circumstances were the peddlers allowed to sell intoxicating liquors, food which was not fresh, or to purchase scrap or other "junk," as it was called, from workers in the camp. Once the application was submitted and signed by officers of the City, the contractor decided to issue or deny the permit. By 1909, only 13 permits had been issued.[40]

That year, on a hot July day, a peddler by the name of William Singer, who owned a store in Shokan but apparently did not have a permit, attempted to enter the camp to deliver clothing which had been ordered. When he refused to stop at the entrance to the camp, he was arrested and detained by a deputy sheriff, who had already arrested and released a baker and a milkman that day. In the ensuing trial, which Singer demanded and at which he pleaded "not guilty," Singer maintained that his customers paid rent to live in the camp, and thus had the right to purchase merchandise from whomever they wished and have it delivered. He also claimed that the road he had used to enter the camp was temporary, and that it could be used by the public according to the law. The jury deliberated for only five minutes, returning a verdict of "not guilty." And so it seemed "home rule" had triumphed over what was perceived to be the greed and imperiousness of the City and its contractor. But that very morning on which the case was being heard, MacArthur and Winston had erected a locked gate at the entrance to the camp. Unaware of the court's decision or the existence of the new gate, another peddler, Samuel Silverstein, soon thereafter, approached the camp in his delivery wagon, which contained an order of meat. He was surprised to see the gate and to be denied admittance. Undaunted, however, he immediately drove his rig up in front of the gate and refused to move, effectively preventing other conveyances from entering the camp unless he did so. Soon, 12 carts were pulled up; the company officials were alerted; and a large crowd congregated. But still Silverstein refused to move. At quitting time, he and his horse and the now spoiled meat remained steadfastly at the gate. As did Singer, Silverstein believed—and the court agreed with him—that commerce could not be restricted between the community and the camp, nor access to highways and public roads be prevented. Thus, in these instances, the seemingly unlimited power of the City and the contractor was tested and limited.

The camp itself, which Chief Engineer Smith had estimated would cost the contractor, with the plant, 1-1/2 million dollars to build, was constructed in a semicircle below the dam along the Esopus Creek on the southerern slope of Winchell Hill near Brown's Station. It was actually a modern village, containing many of the conveniences of a small city, including running water, electricity, paved and lighted streets, sewer pipes, a sewage disposal plant, and garbage and ash collection. The camp had been laid out from the beginning in an orderly pattern of streets, each named for various engineers, commissioners, and other public officials, who had contributed their efforts to the project. Names such as Burr, Freeman, Stearns, Shaw, Chadwick, McClellan, and Gaynor graced the many street signs. In addition to nearly 200 multi-room dwellings, many of them rough boarded four-room cottages, 16 x 40 feet, which were reserved for married men and their families and sold for $400 without sewer and water, there were seven dormitories, eight barrack buildings, and also a kitchen and dining hall; a restaurant; hospital; bakery, which baked 5,000 loaves of bread a day; a commissary; shoemaker and barbershops; storehouses, stables housing over 200 mules, which had been brought to Kingston from Virginia on specially built barges; an icehouse; and a bank capitalized at $25,000 and operated by the contractor.[41] In addition, there were offices, three schools, a firehouse and police station, a post office, three churches, and a bandstand.[42] Smaller camps, such as the East Dike Camp, the East Portion Middle Dike Camp, and the South Wing Camp, were maintained at other points convenient to the work.

These camps were places of vitality and variety. The many different nationalities and ethnic groups which inhabited them came from all over Europe as well as from 27 of the United States, and invested the environs with a richness of life and color characteristic of each group's cultural idiosyncrasies. This created a human tapestry strikingly different from the accepted pattern of life lived by the locals, who at times were shocked by what they saw. In this regard, it was the custom during the first years of the work at the dam for locals to drive to the camp on Sunday in order to view their odd, new neighbors. There were blacks who had journeyed north from the rural South to drive the big wagons hauled by mules. Mrs. C. S. Bergner, who as a child had lived at the camp, remembers how at quitting time at 5 P.M., after hearing the familiar company whistle, all children knew that they must get off the roads leading to the mule barn; for the "chariot race" between the three-mule teams, would soon be taking place, their black drivers standing up, cracking their long whips for effect. In delight, the children "whooped and waved," and mothers often stood on their cottage porches to watch the spectacle.[43]

It was an especially difficult time for blacks in American history. The years 1903, 1906, and 1908 were marred by major race riots. One-third of all blacks living in the North were illiterate. And little serious thought was given to the issues of equality or integration. Some people even believed that blacks were not American citizens. Sadly, two popular songs of the time, which referred to blacks, were unashamedly entitled, "Honey, Stay in Your Own Backyard" and "Every Race Has a Flag but the Coons." Locals, being less familiar with blacks, or "colored," as they were called, many never having seen so many blacks gathered together at one time, seem both to have shunned and feared them. In December of 1908 when the Presidential investigation took place at Ashokan, there were 123 American blacks at work on the project. These men were segregated into living quarters separate from the foreigners and the American whites. No one, at the time, except the blacks, thought anything of this shameful state of affairs.

Also at work were Russians, Slavs, Rumanians, Lithuanians, and Poles; Swedes, Finns, and Danes; Hungarians, Austrians, and Germans; as well as Irishmen, who worked at clerical jobs, piloted steam shovels, or acted as policemen; one Canadian, one Englishman; and a Greek. The most numerous group of foreign workers by far was the Italians. At any one time they constituted 1/2 or more of the entire work force. The Austrians, and then the Russians, in that order, made up the other largest groups. Together, however, they only totalled about 6% of the men at work on the dam. After the contractors had placed their bids, Congress had ended the ten-hour work day, passing the "Eight-Hour Law," and this fact may have influenced MacArthur and Winston to rely so heavily on foreign labor, especially Italian. In this regard, it was believed that the Padrone System had been outlawed on New York City public works projects, but this was not so. For this large number of Italian men, mostly young and single, who could neither speak nor write English, were brought directly to the company office in Ashokan from the steamships docked in New York. It was even said that some of these men were criminals, but this is difficult to substantiate. Nonetheless, these men were accompanied by "chaperones," who signed them up, while the men waited outside the company office. At the camp, they lived in barracks, where at night they could be heard singing songs of "the Old Country," accompanied by guitars and concertinas. Many of these men attended a night school maintained by the Italian Immigrant Society, in order to learn the English language, as well as American laws and customs. One of these workers, when interviewed by a young newspaper reporter from the *Tribune*, responded happily, "Fine! Fine! Me lika school, oh, too much." Some workers felt so positive about this new country and its many opportunities that they eventually became naturalized citizens, a few remaining in the area, some settling temporarily in nearby Tongore (now called Olivebridge). Churches and benevolent organizations from New York City also provided light cultural activities, such as concerts and plays, and stocked a library, which carried as well as books, foreign and local newspapers. Father James P. O'Brien, who spoke Italian, was assigned to the camp by Archbishop Farley of New York, who visited the camp himself. The favorite activity of these men, however, was said to be card playing, which only ceased Sundays, when cockfights were held behind the machine shed. On pay day, the Italians could be seen standing in long lines outside the post office, waiting to send money home to their families overseas. The smell of garlic and long "hero" sandwiches, the sight of homemade spaghetti hung out to dry on clothes lines and fences, and the hollow wooden sound of boccie balls hitting each other on the many courts built in front of the dwellings in which they lived, all came to typify the colorful Italian worker, who was a constant source of interest to the locals. In the summer, Charlie the ice-cream man, who sang the praises of his wares in an Italian tenor voice, was a local favorite. And one Ashokan farmer remembers how, when remarking to an Italian worker one day in the commissary about a pair of shoes the worker was purchasing, which were obviously too big for him, the man responded in broken English that he did so in order to get his money's worth.[44] Another anecdote relates how an Italian was once asked who the first man to come to the United States was. When he answered that he did not know, and then was told that the answer was Columbus, who was an Italian as was the worker himself, he reacted with surprise. "I thought," he responded, "it was Mr. Winston (the contractor)."[45] As these anecdotes indicate, in one respect, the local response toward the Italian worker seems to have been one of amusement, even delight at times, concerning their creative and optimistic attempts to adapt to a new and different culture. There was even respect shown for the highly skilled Italian stonemasons brought to this country by Bonfiglio Perini to build the beautiful bluestone walls along the boulevard around the reservoir (now removed), and to set in place the stone riprapping on the dam and dikes. After Ashokan, Perini expanded his activities, developing a multi-million dollar construction company, which itself built dams and reservoirs in the United States and abroad.

This was not the first time that locals had met and worked with foreign Italians. In the 1870s and 1880s, Italians had been brought to the Catskill Mountains to build the railroad. Then, they had lived and worked under miserable conditions. By 1890, New York City contained 1/2 as many Italians as Naples. And between 1890 and 1925, more than 5 million Italians immigrated to the United States. Although conditions were markedly improved in Ashokan in 1908 from those experienced in the 1890s, the Italians, a great majority who came from southern Italy and Sicily, were still perceived by many locals as being non-white; the epithet "Guinea," denoting one who had come from a country inhabited by natives with black skin, was frequently used to describe him.[46]

In 1909 nearly 3,000 men lived together in the camp—the number was to increase to about 4,000 in the years to follow. And, at times, as might be expected, the relations between them were not always amicable. Sargeants Carmody and Ocker, former Board of Water Supply policemen, describe what they perceived to be the general lawlessness of workers at the Ashokan Dam and along the Catskill Aqueduct during these years:

> Ten thousand men, mostly unskilled laborers, and a wild and desperate lot, dumped suddenly into an unpoliced district, can work a lot of havoc. In 1907 they turned the peaceful Wallkill Valley and Catskill regions of New York State into a roaring camp that echoed to their drunken songs and seethed with banditry, outlawry and murder. Though the brawls and orgies were confined, for the most part, to the workmen's camps, not infrequently men stole away to rob and pillage the isolated farm houses in the district. For ten bloody years the natives lived in constant fear of their lives.[47]

Although they make interesting reading, these lurid memories of a "Catskill Reign of Terror" seem a bit exaggerated in tone, if not also in content. More importantly, though, they pertain almost exclusively to work on the 100 mile long Catskill Aqueduct, which Carmody and Ocker had patrolled. There, many more contractors and men worked, often under considerably less favorable and more dangerous conditions than at the Ashokan Dam. Certainly, policing this entire project was extremely demanding work. And patrolmen, who received the relatively high salary of $75 per month and were led by Chief Patrolman Rhinelander Waldo, did, at times, have their hands full.[48] At the height of the work, a maximum force of 377 patrolmen made over 1,500 arrests a year. By the end of 1918, their testimony had resulted in nearly 5,000 convictions, including seven executions for two murders.

The vast majority of these convictions, however, were made for acts committed south of Ashokan. For the MacArthur and

Winston camp was well-policed and maintained, and considerably separate from the neighboring communities. In contrast to the aqueduct, it would seem that acts of violence in the camp and at the dam site were infrequent and relatively inconsequential, considering the magnitude and duration of the project, as well as the number and variety of men who participated in it. Of course there were disagreements and fights, or "fisticuffs," as these altercations were called. Tempers did flare on hot days, or in the long "Winter of Discontent" of 1908-1909. And fights often broke out during the regularly scheduled baseball games.

Although the drinking of intoxicants was prohibited on New York City property, there were 13 bars between the camp and Stone Ridge, about ten miles away. And in most of these establishments, a worker could refresh himself and find a fight, or even a brawl, if he were so inclined. There were also numerous brothels outside the camp, and these "low dives," as they were called, which were thought to harbor a great army of "riffraff, camp followers, and hangers-on," could also become a source of trouble. At times, it was even necessary to call out the contractor's own force of strongmen to settle heated disagreements, or to quell a potential riot started by Italian workers- who might attack their agent or company about the food served to them in the commissary.[49] In 1914 because of the deteriorating political conditions in Europe, Austrians and Italians often argued in groups, which had to be broken up by the police. In addition, the threat of deportation, if drafted by their respective countries, did little to diminish the tension which developed between these two nationalities.

One of the most notable incidents of violence at the camp, however, concerned neither an Austrian nor an Italian. It was a sensational murder committed in 1909, in which a black worker cut his wife's throat with a knife. Although the hapless man was soon caught, while walking along the Ulster and Delaware Railroad tracks in Arkville some miles west of the camp, and was summarily tried and executed, this murder, unusual for this area, was the talk of the community for some time to come. In this regard, it was not unusual for a local temperence newspaper, the *Ulster Square Dealer*, edited by Stephen A.

Abbey of Kingston, to complain bitterly about the workers, calling them a "low breed of aliens," and castigating their penchant for gambling.[50] Yet, in general, it would seem that the work progressed without undue violence or disruptiuon, and the local community accepted, if with reservation, the presence of this volatile and potentially dangerous new social element.

Certainly, more men were injured on the job than during their unusually long leisure hours. Yet, although public health standards at the project were high, sanitary inspections frequent, as required by the terms of the contract, and all workers were vaccinated before beginning work, and those who later contracted contagious diseases promptly isolated, disease, injury, and death did occur. In 1910, for example, on the entire Catskill Aqueduct project, including Contract 3 at the Ashokan Dam, 321 cases of communicable disease and 86 deaths were recorded. Of these cases, among them typhoid, scarlet fever, diptheria, and tuberculosis, malaria, with 250 cases, was the most prevalent ailment. To combat disease and to treat workers who were sick or injured, the contractors built a hospital and retained the services of trained medical personnel. An ambulance was also kept in readiness, as were first aid kits throughout the camp. A hospital of 23 beds and the attached nurses' cottages were centrally located in the camp, accessible to both the street and the railroad. Contained in the hospital were a doctor's office, a dispensary, vaccination room, preparation room and surgery, and two sun parlors. In attendance were Dr. J. V. Hibbard, the surgeon and head physician, his assistant, Dr. Knapp, and three nurses, including Miss McGee, the head nurse, who once had told a recalcitrant patient, that if his behavior did not improve, she would have him whipped. The average numnber of patients at the hospital was usually about five.

Before the coming of New York City, local country doctors, such as Dr. Williams of West Hurley and Drs. Bloom and Dumond of Shokan had ministered to the medical needs of the inhabitants of the area, often being paid in produce, or even in venison. Traveling on horseback, or by horse and buggy, these medical practitioners offered their services toward the alleviation of a wide range of human complaints. In an era devoid of antibiotics and sulfa drugs, when flu (called the "grippe") could wipe out entire communities, as it did in the winter of 1917-1918 in sections of the Catskills, and when doctors were often inadequately trained, and in some states not even licensed, a patient had a 50%-50% chance of actually being injured by a physician.[51] Amputation, for example, was a common medical practice for treating leg and arm wounds. In addition, there was no satisfactory therapy at the time for diabetes. Herbal remedies were frequently prescribed, prepared, and dispensed by doctors. Catnip tea was given to babies as a sedative. Digitalis and foxglove were administered for "dropsy," or swelling. And cannabis prescribed for menstrual cramps, which were referred to as "cabin fever." Malnutrition, other nutritional deficiencies, and exhaustion from overwork were also common, as was "summer complaint," or diarrhea, for which laudanum was the remedy, sold at local general stores for 10 cents a bottle.[52] Other popular patent medicines, or "elixers" as they were called, purchased by the ailing at the time were Gray's Balsam, which proposed to cure cough and prevent pneumonia, Ayer's Pills, and Castoria for constipation. Locals even sought help, it would seem, from the deleterious side effects of the medication itself, often opium or alcohol-based. Thus, organizations, such as the Manhattan Therapeutic Association, were formed. It guaranteed in its advertisements published in a local newspaper to quickly and effectively cure any form of drug addiction at a reasonable cost.

Considering the contemporary state of medicine and, initially, the lack of programs such as Workmen's Compensation, workers on large public works projects, such as the building of the Ashokan Reservoir, took great risks. Many, in fact, paid a stiff price, being killed or maimed as a result. One local man, who was hired by MacArthur and Winston, caught his gloved hand in the gear of a Monarch steamroller, which he was operating on the north wing of the main dam. When he was brought to the camp hospital, and his mangled hand was examined, the man was horrified to be told by the surgeon that he could only "make some sort of hook out of it." The accident, the worker later said, "tore my poor hand all to hell."

Nonetheless, he survived the operation, and lived for another 72 years as a farmer and revered local historian.[53] Others were not so fortunate. One man named Ben Gray was badly scalded by steam from a dinky train engine, when his locomotive collided with another near the Beaverkill Dike. A number of workers fell to their death, when a scaffold on the lower side of the dam collapsed. Ray Kist, a Pennsylvania "Dutchman," was killed while repairing the stone crusher. Somehow caught by their clothing, he and his assistant were dragged into the machine. Only the assistant survived, but lost both legs. Kist had recently been married. It was also rumored that Swedish workers had been pitched from wagons into the dike and run-over by mules, never to be recovered, and that some 40 blacks and Italians had been killed on the job and buried in unknown graves. In general, however, the death rate on the entire Catskill Water System project was proportionately lower than that of New York City for the same time period. In the City it was 3.5 deaths per 1000 individuals. New York State Labor statistics indicate that in seven years of work (from 1908-1915) on the entire Water System, including Contract 3 at Ashokan, 288 people were killed and 8,839 injured.

Proposed dam site, 1906

Measuring weir, below dam site, 1906

Eight foot conduit used to divert Esopus Creek at dam site.

Dam in various stages of construction

Dam in various stages of construction

North and south wings of dam

Derricks and skips at dam site, blockyard in distance

Winston and Co. railroad bridge, upstream from dam site

The last bucket

Main Plant, north bank, Esopus Creek

The Reservoir filling

Powerhouse with foundations for compressors

Machine shop

Dividing weir

Camp cookhouse, Brown's Station

Workers

Traction engine

Catskill aqueduct shaft

Rivals

Old homestead, Brown's Station

Mountain Gate House, West Shokan

Old Stone Road, East Basin

Abandoned quarry, East Basin

Stone crusher

Bear hunter and boarding house owner Gene Kerr and wife

Rowl Bell and Aunt Becky

Post Office, Brown's Station

Willow Brook House, Brodhead's Bridge

John Burroughs visits Ashokan area where he first taught school

Boulevard circles Ashokan Reservoir

Chapter 6

CLEARING and EXHUMATION

SOME OF THE MOST UNUSUAL, even bizarre, work done at Ashokan entailed the preparation of the land itself for its inundation. This massive job required the disinterring of thousands of bodies buried in local cemeteries and the clearing and grubbing of the vast acreage within the "take line." Even "the dead will not. . .be permitted to rest," stated an illustrated pamphlet published in 1909. Then, it added, all buildings, trees, and other vegetable matter will be either removed and burned, or hauled away. Thus, when man has finished this work, the bed of the Ashokan Reservoir will be "more barren of vegetation than the arid Sahara."[54] In this regard, the disinterment of bodies began during the early stages of construction and proceeded from 1909 through 1911. The clearing and grubbing followed in March of 1912, commencing once the construction of the dam was nearing completion. Both basins of the reservoir were not fully cleared until October of 1914, after a conduit through the dam had been plugged and the water was rising.

On March 30, 1909, the Board of Water Supply took action in reference to the removal of bodies from cemeteries, allowing the sum of $15 to a friend or relative who would conduct the disinterment. An additional sum of $3 was allowed for removing and resetting the headstone. This amount of $18 was soon contested, however; for John Sheldon suggested that a fairer amount would be $85. In response, the City decided that it was cheaper in the long run to settle individual claims out of court than to litigate—a source of annoyance to the Corporation Counsel. And so, the stipend remained the same, although Sheldon won his case. The board also decided that all bodies not removed before November 1, 1910 would be thereafter removed by the Board to a cemetery which it would select, unless before that date some cemetery within 10 miles of the gravesite was designated for reburial by a friend or relative of the deceased. In many cases, relatives, as was their right, designated an "undertaker" to act as their agent in performing the removal. This practice developed a new industry, giving local farmers, stonecutters, liverymen, as well as undertakers, such as Al Schoonmaker of Shokan and Lee Bright of Phoenicia (who also buried the workmen who died at the construction site), a great deal of work. In this matter, the question of possible graft and fraud was frequently raised. In addition, some people had difficulty in filling out the applications for removal, often citing the incorrect relationship of the applicant to the deceased. On one such form, a woman applicant had written "grandmother." This confused the authorities and prompted their request for an explanation; for the plan of the cemetery showed that only the body of a small child was buried there.

Nonetheless, the resolutions of the Board being published, and their conditions advertised, the grisly process was begun. In the reservoir district, there were nearly 40 cemeteries, ranging from isolated graves on farms to public burial grounds containing hundreds of interments. It was realized at an early stage that the removal of bodies was an extremely sensitive subject. And so, the City developed a three-step plan to diminish potential local resistance. First, all known cemeteries were surveyed and all available data secured. This, however, was difficult, in that some cemeteries, such as the Olive Bridge Cemetery, were known by different names. Also, many of the graves in these cemeteries were overgrown with weeds, others entirely obliterated. In some cases, little attention had been paid to the order or arrangements of graves, which faced in all directions. Some graves were not marked with headstones, their presence being indicated only by the uneven contour of the ground.

Others were found with the use of old maps and other historical documents. All identified graves were cleared, staked, and numbered. Second, new maps were prepared showing the exact location on the ground of each grave. A list of names of the deceased was also compiled. Often, in order to obtain some of these names, it was necessary to initiate a house to house canvas, in which old residents were interviewed concerning those buried in the cemeteries of the region. Thus, graves which at first had been designated "Unknown" or "Unlocated" were identified, and in some cases, new locations were discovered, some suggesting that these were the last resting places of murdered people and unwanted babies. After this research, the third step, the actual removal work, was undertaken. In total, some 2,720 bodies were removed from the floor of the reservoir. Of these bodies, most were identified. However, some 368 remained either unknown or unclaimed. By Agreement 81, these bodies were removed from reservoir property in 1911 by Mathias and Alonzo Burgher and Joseph Hill, and reinterred in the Burgher cemetery at the head of Watson Hollow in new West Shokan. A bluestone marker 12 inches high by 12 inches wide, inscribed with two letters indicating the name of the previous cemetery and a serial number for identification, was set at the head of each grave. For many years afterward, some of these cut stones, which had not been used, remained in the area, leaning against trees or laying unused in fields. To this day, however, over 100 bodies, which were recorded in files as having been buried in particular cemeteries, remain unlocated, and thus now rest somewhere beneath the liquid grasp of Ashokan's waters.[55]

To a man who participated in this work, actually exhuming the bodies of his descendants, as well as those of his deceased friends and neighbors, this was "one of the most gruesome, interesting jobs" he ever held.[56] In one grave he found a petrified body of a woman, which reminded him of an Egyptian mummy. He remembers how they had placed a rope under the body, and he had steadied her feet as they raised her from the opened coffin. Most of the bodies, however, were generally piles of bones. These were reburied in rough wooden boxes 3 feet long and 1 foot square. Treatment of these remains, he remembers, was often irreverent, and drinking on the job by the undertakers was not infrequent. Sometimes the workers would sleep in the caskets, or ride in the back of the wagon with the bodies.

The work was not without its humorous moments, however. One woman designated that her second husband should disinter her first husband, who had been dead for only a few years. When her new husband did so, he found the first husband's body in a high state of preservation. Therefore, he removed the body from the coffin and reburied it in another cemetery as requested by his wife. However, he buried the body standing on its head. When asked why he did this, he answered that this man had been the only perfect man who had ever lived, according to his wife. And so, he was getting even with him now.[57] One local farmer vigorously protested against the removal of bodies, calling it "body snatching." But the only funereal thievery seems to have been done by the ubiquitous woodchuck, which unwittingly burrowed into graves and dragged out the bones of a leg or a skull it found in its way.

A great many of the bodies had been buried for many years. Two gravestones in the Olive Bridge Cemetery bore the dates 1740 and 1790, other stones several dates prior to 1807. One corner of the Bloom and Brodhead Cemetery at Brodhead's Bridge was devoted exclusively to the burial of slaves. A black cobbler, who proved descent, removed these bodies under the Board's offer. Other slaves, it was said, having belonged to the Chrispell family, had been buried on the Bishop farm above the flowline of the reservoir. Some cemeteries were even thought to have been ancient Indian burial grounds before being taken over by the white man.[58]

Two stories involving the removal of bodies from the reservoir are of interest. The first involves the Kingston poet Henry Abbey, whose national reputation as a minor poet was notable at the time. Abbey arranged with the Board to have the bodies of his grandparents, Jonathan and Lucy Abbey, removed from the reservoir to the Montrepose Cemetery in Kingston, as was his right. And since the headstone of Lucy's grave was cracked in three places, Abbey took this opportunity to order the cutting of a new stone, on which he changed the inscription. In due time, the bodies were removed and reburied, and the new stone was set, as requested. However, when the poet visited the new grave sometime thereafter, he was shocked to note that everything was not as he had intended. The poetic inscription had been added, as expected, but the headstone bearing that inscription had cracked once again – in three places.[59]

Prior to the construction of the reservoir, and many years before the idea had even been considered, the lovely but delicate daughter of a prosperous local farmer became engaged to be married. Despite her tendency to experience fainting spells in times of stress, plans for the wedding went forward. A beautiful white gown was sewn, and all the previous family heirlooms, a necklace with a locket, a pair of earrings, and a ring were taken out for the bride to wear. People for miles around were invited to the celebration. And mountains of food were cooked. Unfortunately, the day before the ceremony, the young woman had one of her spells, and did not come out of it, as was usual. The doctor was called. His efforts, though, proved in vain, and soon she was pronounced dead. And so, the wedding guests became mourners, as later that day, she was buried in her gown and jewels. That night, two of her friends, who had acted as pallbearers, began philosophizing about the shortness of life, and decided to rescue the jewels from the grave. Certainly, their young friend, they thought, no longer needed them, as they themselves did. Building up their courage, the two men went to the graveyard, removed the loose earth, and raised the lid of the coffin. Moonlight played on the open but unseeing eyes of the beautiful, young woman dressed in her white gown. Conquering their fear, they took the earrings and the necklace, but were unable to remove the ring from her finger. Panicking, one of the men gave the ring a rough tug. The ring came off, but took with it some skin. Then, to their horror, the finger began to bleed, and the woman sat up. The men shreiked, but soon realized what had happened, returning the shivering girl to her surprised parents. The story concludes by relating that the wedding finally took place, the women living to a ripe old age and raising a fine family. As the story is told, when she died, she was buried in the same cemetery as earlier, although in a different grave. Here, though, she found no rest. For once again, she was disturbed a second time by the construction of the Ashokan Reservoir. This time, however, when disinterred, she did not sit up like Lazarus who rose from the dead, as she had done years before. Today, she sleeps peacefully, some say forever, in the Mt. Evergreen Cemetery in Woodstock, New York.[60]

In March of 1912 after all the bodies that could be found were moved, Joseph T. Rice, a partner in the construction company of King, Rice, and Ganey, began the clearing and grubbing of the floor of the reservoir. Rice, a man very different in background from the aristocratic James Winston, had subcontracted this massive undertaking from J. F. Cogan Company, which held Contract 72, amounting to nearly $400,000. Rice was a tall, blue-eyed man, "down-to-earth, a nuts-and-bolts person," according to his daughter.[61] Rice, who in later life was thought physically to resemble Abe Lincoln, had been born in Milwaukee, Wisconsin into a family of nine children; his mother and father were Irish immigrants. Working first as a messenger boy on the railroad traveling from Milwaukee to Chicago, Rice had generously given his entire first month's pay, a gold piece, to his widowed mother. Being extremely strong physically, Joseph later apprenticed himself to a stonemason, and this job led to others in the construction trade. Having taken only six years of schooling from the Irish Christian Brothers, Rice always regretted his lack of formal education, insisting that all his children attend and graduate from college. Throughout his long life of 85 years, he remained an avid and voracious reader. In addition to clearing and grubbing the Ashokan basins, Rice and his company built siphons and completed other work on the Catskill Aqueduct, installed a new sewer pipe (into the Rondout) for the City of Kingston, later grubbed and cleared the village of Gilboa, New York in the Schoharie Reservoir, and built a section of the 8th Avenue Subway in New York City. A friend and great admirer of Chief Engineer J. Waldo Smith, Rice, in his long and lucrative career, later acted as consultant to the Los Angeles Water System. Nonetheless, he considered the Catskill Water System the best in the world, believing it his greatest personal achievement to have participated in the project.

Prior to the clearing, since most of the available data concerning the preparation of reservoir basins had been obtained on projects in New England, where the soil is of a different nature, two scientists named Hazan and Fuller were engaged to run tests on the soil. In the course of their experiments, it was found that the generally clay-like soil in the Ashokan basins yielded up to water quite slowly and was relatively insoluable, being practically stable in character when immersed in water and kept out of contact with the air. Thus, it was determined that little top soil other then that which contained contaminated material, such as found in privies, cesspools, and barnyards, would require excavation. This soil would be removed and the site disinfected with hypochlorite of lime. Primarily, the greatest amount of matter which would require extraction would be the vegetation which grew above the surface of the soil. In this way, the type and extent of treatment of the basins was determined. It was concluded, therefore, that an estimated area of 9,500 acres was to be cleared of brush, trees, houses, and other buildings. 2,400 acres of that total acreage were to be grubbed to a depth of 6 inches of roots and stumps over 2 inches in diameter. Ultimately, however, 10,377 acres were cleared, 1,870 grubbed, and 1,022 cubic yards of material excavated. This work was to be done in swampy areas and in a strip of land 5 feet above and 15 feet below the flow line, in order to create a beach which would be attractive and not covered with unsightly debris driven to shore by wave action.

To accomplish the clearing, Rice and his men used cross-cut saws and an endless-chain saw, run by an automobile engine and mounted on a stone boat, which could be dragged to any relatively level location. Trees less than 6 inches in diameter were cut flush with the ground; larger trees were cut leaving stumps of no higher than 1 foot. Brush and small trees, however, had to be cut twice, since during the 2-1/2 years of clearing, a vigorous second growth sprouted. Salvage obtained from trees—a considerable item—belonged to the contractor and was sold as firewood, lumber, fence posts (locust), fuel for smoking hams (hickory), pulpwood for dynamite (softwoods), and wood for making billiard tables (maple), tool handles (apple and fruit woods), and wood alcohol (hardwoods), and charcoal. All buildings ultimately became the property of the contractor, and were either destroyed or dismantled and sold as building materials. A few buildings were moved. During the act of clearing, some interesting discoveries were made. One tree, which bore the scars of a lightning strike, embraced beneath its roots a mass of fused metal-like substance similar to glass. Another, an old, hoary grandfather of a tree, when it was cut at the sawmill, upon close examination revealed that embedded in it was a flint tomahawk, the result, no doubt, of some Indian hunt or battle in the dim reaches of the past.

The removal of stumps, or grubbing, was done in two ways. The first method employed was to cut the trees several feet from the ground, and then to attach a chain connected by a steel cable to a capstan type stump puller, which was pulled by mules. The second, and more effective method, was to use a Caterpillar traction engine. Since with this machine it was not necessary to cut down the tree first, the cable being attached to the standing tree or trees at any height and thus pulling them down and then jerking them out with their roots attached, the Caterpillar could do a great deal of work in a day. Its record was amazing. It had extracted 50 trees, 8 to 10 inches in diameter, each hour, for a period of four hours. If this pace had been maintained, it would have amounted to the removal by one machine and its crew of approximately 400 trees per eight-hour day, or 2,000 to 2,400 per week. Some trees, as well as certain locations in general, were more difficult to clear and grub than others. The most difficult trees to remove were the large chestnut trees, which had been cut previously and had later sprouted again. It was necessary to remove these stumps with the aid of explosives. On these days, a cloud of black smoke from the blasting cast a pall over the entire valley. Swamps were the most difficult to grub, since the machine required firm ground on which to operate. During such work in the Beaverkill Swamp, stumps were removed, which some believed had been gnawed by the huge teeth of prehistoric beavers.

As the transformation of the floor of the Ashokan progressed, the basins were flooded in stages up to specified levels of elevation to hold down the second growth. This was accomplished by the construction of temporary dikes on the smaller streams feeding the Esopus. Then, when storage of water began in the West Basin in September of 1913 after the main dam was plugged, a log boom, over 1,000 feet long, was strung across the Esopus Creek, in order to gather the mass of floating material which the rising waters had dislodged. A 28-foot motor launch and an 8 foot wide, 3-1/2 foot deep, 18 foot long scow were used to collect this refuse.[62]

To complete this awesome task of clearing nearly 13 square miles and grubbing a shoreline of approximately 40 miles, Joseph T. Rice employed a work force of nearly 400 men. Many of these workers were Russians, who had been met at the boats in New York, and transported directly to the Ashokan. These men did much of the clearing and grubbing work. Trucking, on the other hand, was done by local workers, who often provided their own wagons and teams. Often, up to 30 draft horses were used at one time.

One local man remembers being hired by Rice, who personally supervised the work riding on a big black horse. The local man, then just a boy, but good with horses, had asked Rice for a job. In response, Rice had answered, that down at the clearing there was a team which no one could handle. If the boy could do so, he would get the job. The strapping young man said he would give it a try, and doing so, was successful. "I guess you'll be all right," commented Rice laconically. And so he was, working for Rice not only driving team, but also dismantling and burning his own village of Olive City. When asked years later, when he was in his eighties, what it must have been like to participate in the destruction of his hometown, the man answered matter-of-factly, that there was nothing to be done about it, and that was that. Yet, he was quick to add, somewhat sadly, that the roaring fire which had consumed his childhood home, the sparks shooting like Fourth of July rockets high into the sky, had "torn at his heart strings," as he phrased it, and it was a night he would never forget. "The ashes remained hot for days," he said. He also remembered how people had surreptitiously stripped vacated houses, which earlier had been rented temporarily to their previous owners prior to demolition or movement.[63] Although against the law, this form of vandalism, as it might be called today, or "night work," as it was euphemistically named then, became a popular nocturnal activity. Even some of the men employed by the City itself became actively engaged in this enterprise. And only the rising waters, it seemed, could put an end to it.

Chapter 7

CONDEMNATION and ACQUISITION OF LAND

SURPRISINGLY, some of the inhabitants of Ashokan, when they learned that they must sell their land and leave, were glad.[64] They had their reasons, most often that their land was poor and they could not make a decent living on it. But most reacted to the news with shock and horror. The city had estimated the value of Ashokan property at about $331 per acre across the boards. However, under the law enacted in 1905, the City was given permission to take possession of a parcel of land, including the owner's dwelling and other buildings, at ten days notice, upon the payment of 1/2 the assessed valuation of the property deposited in a local bank. In the first decade of the twentieth century, assessed valuations were low. And thus, property which had a sale valuation of $5,000 might be assessed for $500. Thus the owner would be forced to move upon notice and the payment of the paltry sum of $250. In this regard, a number of the parcels surveyed and condemned had no identifiable owners. One dollar was awarded in each of these cases, such as for Parcels 492, 503, and 531.

It was also a lucrative period for attorneys, called by some "the time they shook the plum tree."[65] It seemed that, once the inevitable loss of property was accepted, almost everyone filed a lawsuit against the City, the resulting litigation lasting nearly 25 years and amounting to 267 volumes of legal documents.

Claimants were represented enthusiastically by local attorneys. Among them were, most notably, A. T. Clearwater, and also Harrison T. Slossen, former Justice John G. Van Etten, Arthur H. Brown, Edward A. Alexander, and William D. Brinnier. For their services, attorneys received 5% of land settlements and 25% of settlements for indirect damages, although the figures had been higher before a Supreme Court decision of 1909 settled the matter and established the lower, and some said fairer set rates. One Kingston lawyer, former State Senator John L. Linson, had amassed over 1/4 million dollars in fees in less than three years. Periodically, nevertheless, attorneys petitioned for a 5% increase in the rates, but to no avail.

Although there had been a provision by which the Board of Water Supply could acquire property by direct agreement with the owners and save the time and expense of the regular condemnation method, as it turned out, this provision proved to be of little help in facilitating the transfer of land. For although the Board of Water Supply had the authority to agree with the property owner on a price, each agreement required the approval of the Board of Estimate. Thus, frequently, the payment was so long delayed, with neither interest nor legal expenses being paid, that the property owner, in the long run, gained nothing by choosing this method. As a result of the bureaucratic inefficiency and the consequent impatience of Ashokan landowners, a considerable amount of land speculation took place. According to the *Pine Hill Sentinel*, in order to obtain ready cash for their land, many landowners sold their land outright or gave options on it to a Tammany Hall backed "land option ring," with a local real estate broker, Frank Burhans, acting as its agent.[66] One member of that group, it was intimated, was a personal friend of the Mayor of New York, George B. McClellan. The *New York American* stated, ". . .a small coterie of shrewd New York real estate operators, with political affiliations have taken title to more than 1/3 of the land to be taken. . . ." The newspaper added that the Syndicate held another 1/3 of the land in option.[67] This "Syndicate," as it was called, purchased land for as low as $20 per acre, and later claimed in condemnation proceedings as much as $200 per acre. Francis Reynolds, for example, sold his 88 acres for approximately $2,700. In turn, the Syndicate asked from the City $13,500, or five times what they had paid for it. Some acreage was also bought on a "contract mortgage basis." In this type of transaction, the Syndicate paid 5% down to the owner, and then an additional 15% six months later. The balance was paid in installments over an agreed upon period of time.

It must be said, however, that the estimate by the *New York American* of Ashokan land held by the Syndicate seems a bit exaggerated. For it would appear that a great percentage of the inhabitants of Ashokan chose to endure the lengthy, but potentially more lucrative condemnation proceedings, rather than sell directly to the Syndicate or the City at the low rates which were offered to those who wanted their money fast, so they could leave the area and start a new life that much sooner. During these condemnation proceedings, a determination as to the price to be paid by the City for the parcel of land was made by a commission appointed by the Board of Water Supply of three men, who each were paid the sum of $50 a day plus expenses. These Commissions, which were appointed, heard testimony from resident appraisers hired by the City, who were known locally as the "City's experts," as well as from claimants and their expert witnesses.

Claimants, if they wished, could hire their own attorneys. Other expenses for those hearings, for transportation and for the testimony of expert witnesses, were paid by the City. Once a determination was reached, the award, if not paid upon settlement, nonetheless, was received by the seller sooner than if he had sold the land by agreement. In addition, by this method the seller also received 6% annual interest on the award, reckoned from the date upon which his determining commission had been sworn in. By the end of 1912, through condemnation and direct purchase by agreement, the City had purchased some 21,138 acres in all.[68] 15,222 acres of that figure lay in Ashokan, and comprised 18 surveyed sections, containing 954 individual parcels of land, situated primarily in the townships of Hurley and Olive, and including the villages and hamlets of West Hurley, Glenford, Ashton, Olive Branch, Brown's Station, Olivebridge, Olive City, Brodhead's Bridge, Shokan, West Shokan, and Boiceville.

In view of the magnitude and complexity of this process of land transfer, it is not surprising that City politicans and newspapers, among these publications the *World* and the *Tribune*, criticized the condemnation proceedings as overly expensive, and not infrequently suggested the possibility of payroll padding and other forms of graft. In fact, in 1910, even Mayor McClellen, who had initiated the Catskill Water System, was replaced by a reform candidate, William J. Gaynor. Once elected, Gaynor promptly went about firing clerks, reducing advertising and other costs, and eliminating, in addition to the office of the Special Counselor himself, thc great numbers of highly paid appraisers. A local headline at the time read, "Plumland Heads Under the Axe."[69] Notwithstanding this drive for economy and reform, when the purchase of the lands at Ashokan was completed, the cost still amounted to nearly 6 million dollars.[70] Of that amount, however, property owners received only $3,622,445. In comparison, the expenses incurred by the City in that purchase were over 2 million dollars. This means that for every dollar paid to a property owner, the City also paid Commissioners, attorneys, witnesses, appraisers, and a myriad of other individuals an aditional 60 cents.[71]

The condemnation hearings were held at the Court House in Kingston, where the crowds were often so large that Sheriff Boice was forced to serve notice that hearings could not be held while court was in session. During these often rambunctious hearings, interesting testimony was taken quite frequently from a parade of colorful witnesses. Millard H. Davis, a Boiceville farmer, often appeared as a witness for local property owners. In one case, he related that a particular property had a brook flowing across it. When asked by Howard Chip, the attorney for the City, if it was a murmuring brook, Davis answered, "No, it's a still, quiet, sylvan brook." In response, Chip asked Davis whether this brook was worth as much as a murmuring brook, and Davis replied, "I think not," but quickly added, that the murmuring brook would be his personal choice anyway. Another local witness, however, Foster Mitchell of Stone Ridge disagreed, saying that he preferred the sylvan brook. Attorney Chip rejoined, referring to Davis, "I always insisted you had more poetry in your nature than Mr.

Mitchell has."[72] In another case, testimony was heard concerning whether a house was on "the dirty side of the street" or not, a matter of singular importance, it would seem, in determining its value.

The awards made to property owners varied. According to one litigant, "Influential people received better awards than small fry, and some commissions gave bigger awards than others. The awards were uneven."[73] The amount of the award, also, seems to have been influenced by the experience and reputation of one's attorney. A. T. Clearwater, for example, was particularly effective in behalf of his local clients. In fact, he represented, among many others, the Ulster and Delaware Railroad, winning a settlement of $2,800,000. William D. Every's 182 acre farm, the "finest in West Shokan," containing the site of an old Dutch blockhouse, was appraised by Millard H. Davis at $52,000. Every claimed $53,000. Oliver Yale, the owner of the 4.378 acre quarry used by MacArthur and Winston and Company as a source of building stone for the dam, claimed the exorbitant figure of $100,000. His settlement, however, was considerably less. Sheriff Boice, somewhat better connected (as might be expected) received $27,545 for his sawmill against a claim of $32,718.24. A descendant of Indian fighter Peter Longendyke and a holder of an original land grant from George III, Mrs. Mary A. Weeks, claimed $10,000 for her property. Although she was represented by A. T. Clearwater, she received as her settlement only $4,900. The largest single award to a property owner was made to John I. Boice, who owned Parcel 22 in Section 1. For this land and the historic gristmill situated at Bishop's Falls, he received $112,000. 14 days were devoted to the presentation of testimony and the deliberation of this claim, in which Boice's witnesses estimated the value of his property at $280,000 and $325,000 respectively. Unfortunately, however, although the original settlement was considerably lower than these local estimates, a month later, as sometimes was the case, even that amount was reduced to $99,600, which Boice had no choice but to accept.

Probably the most interesting and highly publicized claim, however, concerned neither large sums of money, nor a structure of lasting architectural value such as the old gristmill. So unusual is its story, that to this day, a legend remains attached to it—the legend of a church which was stolen. With the coming of New York City to Ashokan, ten religious congregations were forced to move. Among them was the Methodist-Episcopal congregation of Glenford. At first, this congregation was awarded $5,600 for its land and buildings, the latter to be sold for from between $10 to $250 dollars. The parishoners were quick to point out, however, that the church building itself had always been thought to stand within the boundaries of the Ulster and Delaware Railraod, which the rest of the church property adjoined. This act of trespass had been allowed, they said, with the kind permission of the president of the railroad himself, a man who was known far and wide as both charitable and religious. In this regard, once the congregation notified president S. D. Coykendall, of the situation, he obligingly offered the building free to the church, if only the members would cart it away. And so, hitching John Chrispell's yoked oxen to the building, the eager and industrious parishoners, to the amazement of all onlookers, moved the church up and out of the Ashokan basin. When the city officials discovered that the church building, which they had considered City property, had vanished, seemingly overnight—actually the removal took the better part of five days—they demanded that it be returned. For as they averred, and their surveyors substantiated, only 1/2 of the building had rested on railroad property. Nonetheless, the congregation refused to accept the City's position and stood firm. In due course, they were cited for trespass and sued for damages, an act which scandalized the community and increased local anger toward the City of New York. Subsequently, on December 8-9, 1914, after the basins had been flooded and all trace of the old church foundations lost forever, the case was tried, A. T. Clearwater representing the trustees of the church, and the local newspapers expending considerable energy in coverage of the affair. Surprisingly, or so it seemed to the trustees, the court ruled in favor of the City, awarding it damages. But nonetheless, the Glenford congregation did retain possession of its hardwon church building, and most everyone was satisfied, the letter of the law having been followed. And so, for the amount of only $45, the church, that to this day some say had been stolen, was allowed to remain at the base of Ohayo Mountain in new Glenford, where it had been moved, another example of the fact that God, indeed, works in mysterious ways.

Chapter 8

BUSINESS and INDIRECT DAMAGES

IN ADDITION to being compensated for the loss of their property, the inhabitants of Ashokan believed that they also deserved recompense for damages regarding the loss of income. Their claims in this regard included business, indirect real estate (decrease in value of land not taken), wage, and diversion (diversion of stream water) claims. At first, the City refused to recognize claims of this sort. It was not until cases such as those of John Rainey, Sam Thompson, and Delancey N. Matthews were tested in the higher courts, that New York City was forced to address the issue of indirect damages, and a Bureau of Claims was established. John Rainey, in addition to the value of his land and the buildings on that land, had also claimed the estimated income he would lose from the loss of his boarding business. Sam Thompson, an employee at Sheriff Boice's sawmill, claimed $235.50 in wages lost during the 157 days it took him to find another job. And D. N. Matthews, a prominent citizen of West Shokan and the owner of a general store, proved with the help of his accurate records, that his business had netted over $80,000 in ten years. He contended that, in justice, he should be paid for the loss of such a lucrative and long-standing business.

From the first condemnation hearings, Kingston attorneys had fought long and hard, in cases of this sort, for the admission of testimony regarding the structural value of buildings taken, the potential use of a parcel for the development of waterpower, and its "availability" as a reservoir site. Initially, claimants were not even allowed to testify in their own behalf.[74] Once Damage Commissions were appointed, however, matters improved for local businesspersons—but not immediately. In that few rules or precedents governed the conduct of these early claims hearings, the tiresome and acrimonious process often dragged on for years. At one point, even A. T. Clearwater, an attorney for claimants, was asked by the commissioners his views concerning the best method to be pursued in the investigation and determination of damage claims. So confused was the situation, and so pervaded with bad feelings, delay, and complications, that years after the completion of the Ashokan Reservoir, millions of dollars in claims were still pending.

Sometimes, before a settlement was reached, the claimants died. This was the situation in the case of Mrs. Tina Lasher. Mrs. Lasher, a widow, had operated a boarding house for some time at Brown's Station on a choice piece of property of about 20 acres situated near the railroad depot. This business had been her only source of income with which to support herself and her son. From it she had received in the summer $6 per week, not including meals, from each 10 to 15 people whom she boarded. At the hearing, Mrs. Lasher had estimated that her expenses included $3.50 per week for the help of a maid, $20 per week for groceries, $40 per year for taxes, and $100 per year for repairs. To supplement her food supplies, she noted, she kept a cow and planted a big garden. Unfortunately, Mrs. Lasher had not kept detailed records, as had D. N. Matthews. And as a result, after numerous appeals and the passage of many years, as a settlement for the loss of her boarding business, for which she had claimed $10,000, Mrs. Lasher's executors, in 1915, received the sum of $1,445, a figure which her attorney, Harrison T. Slosson, said amounted to "a confiscation of her property."[75]

Extensive testimony, much of it sensational, was heard in the case of 70-year old Emma Cudney of Shokan. Represented by A. T. Clearwater, Mrs. Cudney owned the largest ginseng plantation in the Ashokan basin. And ginseng, the harvesting of which supplemented many local incomes, was not only a highly profitable crop, selling for as much as $6 to $7 a pound in

1909, it was also a substance whose very name evoked thoughts of the mysterious Orient. In that ginseng root was believed by the Chinese to possess certain impressive powers as a mild stimulant and as an aphrodisiac, this case, and others like it, generated testimony of a titillating nature, thus pleasing the large crowds at the court house and the avid readers of the local tabloids. According to a noted botanist of the time, Dr. F. G. Carpenter, the Chinese regarded ginseng root as "the greatest medicine on the face of the earth."[76] Each year, it was revealed in the course of the hearing, China purchased over 1 million dollars worth of Catskill ginseng, said by some to be the best in the world. Nonetheless, although a staggering amount of interesting expert testimony was amassed in this case, Mrs. Cudney, whose plantation contained over 20,000 plants, each plant producing for many years both extremely valuable seeds and roots, was awarded only $8,707.50. This was a sum which many considered unfair.

Throughout the hearings, the City maintained the position that the construction of the reservoir had not only not hurt business, it had actually benefited it. To support this contention, the City indicated that many of the displaced residents had remained near by, that new villages had developed, and that over 400 new buildings had been constructed in the immediate area outside the basins.[77] All this activity was evidence, the City stated, of a heightened business climate. Nonetheless, 1/2 of the indirect damage claims made against the City were given awards. These awards, however, most made between 1914 and 1918, usually represented only a fraction of the amounts claimed, often about 20% to 25% of the claim. Most awards amounted, in fact, to only a few hundred dollars. In justice to the City, though, it must be said that some claims were unfounded, or were made by individuals whose businesses were conducted outside of the "taking." Many of these claims were dismissed, or later withdrawn, while others, after consideration, were never submitted.

William J. Green received $500 for the loss of his combined barbershop and sporting goods business. Mary Wolven, a dressmaker, was awarded $300, as was 61 year old Henry Berryann, a cobbler of Olive Branch. Laundresses, such as Amelia

Moss of Brown's Station and Henry Berryann's wife Rovina, usually received about $225 for their washing and ironing businesses, having charged their boarding customers the sum of $1.50 per load. Carpenters, painters, and general contractors, such as Isaac Weeks of West Shokan, John Secor, Alexander Peacock, Milton Nichols of Brodhead, and Martin Slover, all received about $300 each for their respective losses of business. At that time, a carpenter earned the daily wage of about $2.50. Arena Elmendorf, the widow of William Elmendorf who died intestate, was awarded, after appeal, the full amount of $355 settled upon her husband's fish business. Mr. Elmendorf had sold Hudson River shad in Shokan, for which he had paid in Kingston from $28 to $40 a wagon load. Byron J. Baker received $1,000 for the loss of his country store, and Benjamin Giles only $75 for his inventory of masonry supplies. John Gallagher owned a livery business near the Olive City Post Office, and although his claim for the loss of his livery business was dismissed, he was awarded $300 compensation. For Mr. Gallagher was also a noted local musician, who entertained at dances throughout the area. He had been paid, he testified, $3 to $5 per night for his services, his gross receipts for one year amounting to from $500 to $600 dollars. When he had worked, this musician stated, he had had no major expenses. For as he said, "I had a horse of my own." And "They fed me wherever I went." Sometimes he had traveled to the job on the Ulster and Delaware Railroad and then used the rig hired at the station which would be provided for him, as well as his railroad ticket, free of charge. Gallagher had practiced this happy occupation for 20 years, playing the accordion, sometimes accompanied by violin and piano. Due to the decline of the boarding house business, however, calls for Gallagher's services had declined dramatically. At the time of the hearings, he was out of work.[78]

Physicians also filed claims. Dr. De Ver O. Williams, a surgeon in practice in West Hurley since 1885, claimed $20,000 for his 912 patient practice, but was awarded $4,500. His patients had been scattered by the coming of the City, and Dr. Williams had been forced to move. First, he had gone to Claverack in Columbia County across the Hudson River, he testified, but found the competition too great. Then, he had moved to New Jersey, and later to Highland Falls near Newburgh, where he could not make expenses. Finally, he had set up practice permanently in Harrison, New York in Westchester County. Dr. Berton B. Bloom of Shokan, after a distinguished practice of 35 years, settled for $5,500. Dr. DuMond of West Shokan received only $1,500, when his settlement was reduced after appeal.[79]

Both Wilson Hamilton, a trapper, and William Colvin, a quarryman, received no settlements. Hamilton's case was dismissed, because it was averred that he regularly trespassed in his line of work. Colvin's was dismissed, also, because he did not own the quarry he worked. Nonetheless, the testimony in Colvin's case is interesting. Colvin stated that for a seven to eight ton load of bluestone, cut by himself, loaded, and personally delivered by wagon to Wilbur on the Rondout Creek below Kingston, he received the sum of $18. Granting the seasonal nature of his trade, Colvin estimated that his yearly income from quarry work had been about $300.[80] Mattie C. Davis, who had owned a grove for picnic and "excursion parties" and sold homemade maple syrup, was awarded $50, as was Elizabeth Douglas of West Hurley for her honey business. And finally, Millard H. Davis of Boiceville, whom we have met before, received $975 in damages. In addition to his frequent appearances as appraiser and expert witness, Mr. Davis had owned a boarding house and raised apples for 25 years, shipping 500 barrels a year to Europe. Davis, in his inimitable fashion, pointed out at his hearing, that he made more money from apples than from boarders. This, of course, was a distinction which few men in Ashokan could claim.[81]

Chapter 9

CONSTRUCTION COMPLETED

THE FIRST MASONRY for the dam had been laid on September 19, 1908 about one year after the contract had been awarded. And by the end of the following year, the City held title to all lands within the Ashokan basin. General Superintendent J. F. Ham and Department Engineer Carlton E. Davis had kept the thousands of men at work, at times around the clock, on Sundays, and during the winter, whenever the weather had permitted, thus completing 26% of Contract 3. The masonry section of the big dam, which would rise to 252 feet, was 80 feet above the level of the Esopus Creek. The core walls were up to 25 to 30 feet of their planned height, and the Middle, East, and West Dikes were practically completed. Seven million cubic yards of earth and 1 million cubic yards of masonry would be used in the construction of these dikes and the dam before they were finished, enough concrete to bury the Stockade area of nearby Kingston to a depth of 2,000 feet.

While 1909 was the high point of activity and optimism at the construction site in Ashokan, typified by the resounding success of the first transcontinental airplane flight that year, in contrast, 1910 seems a year of uncertainty. The McClellan administration, a strong supporter of the Catskill Water System, had ended, and the new mayor, William Gaynor, had called for an extensive review of the project, initiating a sweeping investigation. At this time, it was predicted by pessimists that the entire project would be stopped. The year, in fact, had begun poorly. On April 26 and 27, heavy spring rains had caused severe flooding in the lowlands below the dam, reminding some of the Johnstown flood of 1889. As a result, the historic Bishop's Falls bridge upstream of the dam had been floated off its moorings and had crashed into the partially completed dam. The following month, the workers had stood and stared with rapt attention at the appearance of Halley's Comet to the southwest over South Mountain. Some of the more superstitious workers had said it was a portent of disaster. Then, on August 9, in an unusually dry summer, as if to prove the truth of their dire forecast, Mayor Gaynor was shot in the neck by a city dockworker, whom the mayor, in an act of fiscal reform, had recently discharged. Although the new mayor survived this wound, his attempted assassination further placed the fate of the Catskill Water System in jeopardy. Inhabitants of Ashokan that summer, however, were more shocked by the sensationalized local murder trial of stockbroker Victor Seydel, a friend of A. T. Clearwater. In addition, their concern was directed towards a consideration of New York City's unsuccessful attempt to dodge payment of the property taxes it now owned on the land it had acquired. Nevertheless, the work on the reservoir generally continued unabated, with nearly 1/2 of the dam completed, as well as all dikes, pressure conduits, the upper gate chamber, the waste weirs, the channel, and the intake of the aqueduct.

The year 1911 saw the continuation of drought conditions, with doubt rising in some minds about the viability of the Esopus and the Ashokan Reservoir as a constant source of water. The Ulster and Delaware Railrad position, that its tracks could not be moved until its claim was paid, was upheld in the courts. And Mayor Gaynor finally completed his cost-cutting and general housecleaning. In September, the prestigious New York State Historical Association, its members guided by the ubiquitous A. T. Clearwater, held its annual meeting at Brown's Station near the Ashokan Dam, which was now 2/3s completed. Clearwater, who had initially fought the project and was, at that time, presenting the claims of dispossessed property owners against the City, rose to the occasion, as was his custom, and grandly stated that the dam was one of the wonders of the Twentieth Century. Participants at this meeting viewed this architectural marvel from the comfort of a private Ulster and Delaware Railroad car. As if to give evidence of the progress that had been made, Winston and Company began to move its large machinery from the plant near the dam, and the Yale Quarry was temporarily closed. The Bower Construction Company, under Contract 59, prepared the foundation for the roads to be built around the reservoir, and Harrison and Burton Company began work on the impressive Traver Hollow Bridge near Boiceville.

In the following year, 1912, the clearing and grubbing in the West Basin was nearly finished, the cemeteries moved, and work on the dam was proceeding day and night, as it neared completion. Plans, also, were made for the eventual plugging of the 190 foot conduit, which carried the waters of the Esopus Creek through the dam.

The year 1913 heralded great changes in Ashokan. The newly organized New York Telephone Company, a consolidation of the old Hudson River Telephone Company and the Citizens' Standard Telephone Company, completed the construction of a telephone line along the north shore of the reservoir, putting that line into service in March and removing the old lines from within the basins by July. The Ulster and Delaware Railroad, in stages, removed its tracks and other property from the basins, and completed the laying of new tracks on the north shore, running the first train over the new line on June 8, entirely completing the work of dismantling the abandoned line by October 28. This removal of vital services, however, was not the only activity taking place in Ashokan during the spring and summer of 1913. Although many of the inhabitants had moved already and were building houses and starting new businesses elsewhere, between 800 and 900 people still remained within the "take line," renting the homes from the City which they had once owned, and expecting any day the final order for evacuation.

Contemporary photographs show a picture of desolation and ruin, with the few remaining houses sad and empty like unlit jack-o'-lanterns, and the land appearing as if a conquering army had recently marched through the territory. Mrs. Ella Lockwood Loomis, a columnist for the Kingston *Daily*

Freeman, chronicled these final days of old Ashokan. "People who knew every foot of this section," she wrote in the spring of 1913, "find themselves lost when they go to Brown's Station and Olive City; with all the land cleared and the houses gone, they have to inquire their way around."[82] The Saint Patrick's Ball, the last dance at the Pythian Hall in West Shokan, and the final service at the Shokan Reformed Church were held in May. In response, Mrs. Loomis commented, "No one really realized what the blotting out of a village meant—until now."[83] In a later article Mrs. Loomis continued, "Very few buildings are left now to be burned. The trees are all cut down and the village fading as a dream. It's a sad regret to many, for the associations centered there were dear and will not easily be forgotten."[84]

Finally, the order for evacuation was announced, and the migration began. The blasting and burning of stumps continued non-stop, and the Winston and Company trains chugged in and out of the reopened Yale Quarry and creaked over the Esopus trestle, as the inhabitants of Ashokan packed their bags and left. By late summer, the villages of Shokan and West Shokan, the largest and most populous, were abandoned, the rented buildings deserted, soon to be burned or dismantled. To the occasional traveler, the villages of Ashokan looked like ghost towns. Then finally, all trace of them was gone. As one observer described the scene, ". . .the West basin was a barren waste, with only stone walls and gaping cellar holes. . . . Not a chimney was left standing."[85]

In this area alone there had been 504 dwellings and three times that number of barns, shops, and outbuildings. There were 9 blacksmith shops, 35 stores, 10 churches, 10 schools, 7 sawmills, and 1 gristmill. There were general stores, meat markets, millinery and watch repair shops, a print shop, photographer's studio, harness and wagon shops, an excelsior mill, stone "docks," a creamery, a heading mill, barber and cobbler shops, bowling alleys, recreation halls, and the many boarding houses. These, too, were now gone: Bessie Jones' Willowbrook in Brodhead's Bridge, which could house 150 guests; the Krom farm in Shokan, once a fresh air farm for tubercular children from New York City; Wank's Park House and the Hamilton

House, built in 1870, in West Shokan; the Cool Breeze; Browns; and the numerous other smaller boarding houses, among them the Maple Cottage, Sylvan Lake, Bishop's Falls House, and the Grandview, closed their doors never to open them again. In 1917, a few years after the clearing of the reservoir, Gene Kerr, a disgruntled boarding house owner commented, "Oh, if somebody would only come along and start something! Ever since the waterworks was started, the valley's been dead—no summer people, nobody to sell butter and eggs to. And it's a beautiful place, too."[86]

By late August, the last of the inhabitants had moved, Oranzo Giles, the eccentric, astrologer storekeeper among them. Others had endured, also, waiting to the last minute. A man named Lord, who housed his large and growing family in an old schoolhouse he had purchased, refused to sell his land to the City, stating that he could find no comparable habitation. In the final days of the clearing, according to his daughter Edna, Lord could holdout no longer, it becoming too dangerous. For the family had been "blasted out," as his daughter describes these terrifying final days, the roof of their house full of holes, the rain coming in.[87] Another woman, Mrs. Ferris Davis, remembers ruefully, "New York City just washed us away."[88] It is interesting to note that about 80% of the inhabitants—nearly 2,000 permanent residents—who were forced to move, were so attached to the area, even as changed as it appeared, that they remained within 25 miles of their old homes, 1/3 around the reservoir and 1/4 in Kingston.

Things, however, were by no means the same. Buildings and highways can be moved at will, but communities cannot. It was said at the time, that although the City had brought jobs and money, it had taken the heart of the land, the most desirable part, and left the inhabitants the rim.[89] In the few short years that it had taken to construct the reservoir, the economic base of the area had been changed irrevocably. At the turn of the century, 85% of the male population of Ashokan considered themselves at least part-time farmers. Thousands of acres of land had been, at some time, under cultivation in the basins. However, after the reservoir was built, farming in any significant measure, ceased to be a viable source of income, as did the boarding house business and its related services. Doctors, shopkeepers, and other essential service people moved away. The post offices and the railroad, whose 13 miles of track had once passed through the center of these towns, connecting them with the outside world, were shifted to the less inhabited north shore of the reservoir. Before this change, an inhabitant of Ashokan could take one of the many trains a day which went to Kingston. His cost was $1.02 for the round trip, which took about 1/2 hour each way. Thus began the pattern of rural isolation and disunity which continued for at least a decade. Certainly, rapid changes were taking place across America prior to World War I, and Ashokan, as well as other rural areas could not remain immune to them. Nonetheless, an old successful way of life, rooted in unanimity of purpose and the shared values of self-sufficiency and community, had come to an abrupt and disrupting end. And thus, a place that had once been called "home," a place which had been tended lovingly for generations, disappeared and was lost forever.

On September 9, 1913 at 6:05 P.M., storage of water in the West basin began. First, a sluice gate was closed on the 6 foot culvert, which had been constructed near a small concrete dam a few feet upstream of the main dam. Second, the filling and sealing, section by section, of the large conduit which cut through the big dam, began, continuing into the next year. The concrete for this stage in the plugging of the dam was mixed in a small plant located at the downstream face of the dam. Just as the transcontinental flight of 1909 had typified the progressivism of that year's work on the dam, the adoption by the Ford Motor Company of the assembly line in 1913 continued the spirit of efficiency and productiveness which the plugging of the dam represented.

At the time the filling began, the Esopus Creek was flowing only at a rate of 22 cubic feet per second; for the summer had been dry, the drought affecting private clubs in the Catskills, such as Twilight Park, where the shortage had reached critical proportions. Local farmers, who had complained about the poor condition of the roads around the reservoir and had threatened to file an injunction against the City, if something were not done to improve them, turned their attention toward the waters, which seemed to be stalled. They humorously suggested that the City should purchase some of this scarce commodity through the Sears and Roebuck catalog. Others said that the bottom of the reservoir was porous, and it would take some sort of expensive compound to caulk the leaks. Certainly, it seemed like the reservoir would never fill. Then, just after Bishop's Falls, proudly advertised in a 1906 Ulster and Delaware Railroad tourist pamphlet, was completely submerged, and the flats between Brodhead's Bridge and the Olive Bridge Dam were covered, the first in a series of fall storms occurred, dropping over 4 inches of rain on the Catskills in 48 hours. This deluge quickly increased the flow of the Esopus Creek to 800 cubic feet per second, effectively stopping all further local criticism. By September 24, a bit over two weeks after the gates had been closed, the water had reached an elevation of 484 feet above sea level, and 1,200 million gallons had been impounded. After this first storm, the flow gradually deceased until October 19, when the water reached 506 feet above sea level, and 3,300 million gallons had been impounded. The following day, a storm of 19 hours duration raged, and a flow of 2,120 cubic feet per second raised the water level quickly to 518.5 feet. This storm was closely followed by another four days later, which increased the flow to 14,000 cubic feet per second by late October, raising the water to the level of the West Shokan bridge and the bottom of the West Inlet channel, thus filling the West basin to over 1/2 of its capacity. At this time, water was "wasted" through the various gate-chamber inlets and channels; debris was cleared away from the dam by the Board of Water Supply boat *Noah's Scow*, and to the amazement of local anglers, huge brook trout were found lodged in the screen chamber. On November 8 the fiercest of all storms lashed the Catskills, with nearly 7 inches of rain falling in the Moonhaw in the mountains above West Shokan, and the flow at the dam increasing to an unprecedented 26,600 cubic feet per second. During the storm, water being wasted through the regular channels passed through the West Dike temporary railroad tunnel, leaked into the aqueduct, and flooded Brown's Station, washing out a portion of the public highway. As one inhabitant who experienced this storm stated, the reservoir at the time was "like a raging sea."[90]

Upstream, the Winston railroad line to the Yale Quarry, which had been nearly repaired since it had been submerged in a previous storm, was inundated once gain, but no major damage was done. However, driftwood had lodged against the big iron bridge across the Esopus at Shokan, lifting it from its pilings. Soon thereafter, no trespassing signs appeared, generating rumors that the planking of the bridge had been secured purposely by the City to its steelwork to assure the destruction of the bridge, and thus to terminate the traversing of reservoir property. On December 12, 1913, water in the West basin reached a maximum elevation of 510.5 feet, impounding nearly 2,700 millon gallons available for use.

On June 19, 1914, the Winston and Company whistles blew for an entire hour; for the major portion of the work on the dam and dikes, except for the facing and completion of the upper parts, had been finished. For two years, however, the impounded water was used only for flushing and for testing the system. Not until nine months after the impounding of water began in the East basin, when the West Hurley Dike had been found to leak and had to be patched, was water sent south to the Kensico Reservoir, ultimately being delivered to the distribution pipes of New York City. At this time, both basins of the Ashokan Reservoir contained over 55 billion gallons of water, or 42% of capacity.

In the following year, 1916, with a decreased labor force and the specter of war appearing on the horizon, Winston and Company finished the dividing weir, the spillway channel, the embankments of the dikes, and the wings of the dam. Earlier in this year, however, disaster had struck the camp, when the company mule barn had burned to the ground, killing 87 mules. It had been a bitterly cold February night, remembers railroad engineer Ed Avery. Avery had been at work repairing a company locomotive next to the big mule barn, when the fire had broken out. He rushed to the barn, but it was too late to go inside and attempt to rescue the panicking animals, the fire being intensely hot. Some of the terrified beasts had already been led to safety and others had run from the barn on their own, their skins scorched and smoking. Most of these unfortunate animals died afterwards. The next day their carcasses were found throughout the camp. These were gathered and buried in a long, deep trench dug in the ballfield, which later became the site of a tree nursery. The fire and its aftermath was a horrible sight, remembers Avery, one he would never forget.

With the finishing touches having been put on the dam and dikes, the last of the workers began to leave Ashokan. As one witness, a little girl at the time, describes the scene, "The camp began to look like a ghost town. . . ."[91] What equipment remained at the site was removed, and the last of the plants was dismantled. The Yale Quarry, a place which had been so actively used for years, fell silent. Weeds and white birch trees began to take root in the tailings and at the base of its dark stone cliffs where the sound of blasting and cutting had echoed for nearly a decade. Even the tracks of the Winston and Company railroad which had serviced it were taken up. Finally, the large and bustling camp, which had housed the many men of different races, creeds, colors, and nationalities, men who had worked together to construct this shining, white dam which rose magnificently like a Roman monument, was unceremoniously razed. Its roads were plowed up, pipes and sewers removed, pipe holes filled in, and the entire area reforested and landscaped. Little trace of this "city in the Catskills" now remains. The tooting of the company railroad donkey engines stopped, and the craking of the derrick cables over the dam, once removed, ceased. The company whistle blew for the last time, and then was taken to a Rondout boatyard, where Liberty ships were being built. In September, the dam was opened to traffic, as was the complete system of roads and bridges around the reservoir a month later. On December 20, 1916, 9 years, 3 months, and 24 days after the awarding of Contract 3 for the main dam of the Ashokan Reservoir, the work was officially completed.

Quickly, interest shifted away from Ashokan. For even before the dust had settled on the great dam, plans were being made to develop the water resources of other sections of the Catskills. Pursuing its need for an unlimited source of water, New York City proposed to join the Schoharie Reservoir to the

Ashokan Reservoir by means of a tunnel dug underneath the intervening mountains to Shandaken on the upper Esopus Creek. Schoharie water would then flow into the Ashokan Reservoir, greatly increasing the available supply. But that is another story. And in the fall of 1917, jubilation over the completion of the work at Ashokan was occurring some 100 miles south in the City. Here, for as far back as the previous century, eyes had turned toward the northwest in the hope of procuring an everlasting source of pure water. Through the magic of modern engineering, this eternal fountain, it seemed, had been found. And so the great celebration took place in New York City, not in Ashokan. Commemorating the "Good Gift of Water," as it was called, schoolchildren danced a rain dance; politicians gave speeches and presented medals, and a special exhibition of Hudson River paintings was displayed. At the dramatic moment, with all awaiting expectantly, New York Mayor Mitchel turned the valve; a jet of long-awaited upstate water shot high into the air, and everyone cheered. The dream of many foresighted New Yorkers had come true. In only two decades from the submission of the report considering water sources west of the Hudson River to the Manufacturers' Association of Brooklyn, the pure and abundant waters of the Catskills, through the combined efforts of public officials, contractors, engineers, and workers, had been brought successfully to the City. This was an act, which even to this day, seems nothing less than a miracle.

Chapter 10

CONCLUSION

IN THE YEARS since the Ashokan Reservoir was built, the local inhabitants have become used to the lake which was created by the big dam, replacing the once familiar valley. The earlier animosity toward New York City has decreased to some extent, as time has passed and as those who personally experienced the change have died. The annual Labor Day reunions of the displaced and their families seem smaller in attendance each year. The deep fear of the dam and the possibility of its disintegration, so strongly felt in 1905, seems completely absent today. To those who live in Kingston downstream, "The Dam" conjures up only positive images of picnicking around the old aerator, now a fountain recently constructed on top of a new hydroelectric plant, the happy prospect of a scenic automobile ride along the Ashokan Boulevard which circles the reservoir, or a walk with one's dog on the Middle Dike, a portion of which has been closed to vehicular traffic for some years. Its old brick road is now apparent beneath the more recent macadam surfacing of the dike, revealing its age of nearly 75 years. Here, photography is popular, and the view of the Catskill high peaks to the west, now called the Burroughs Range after the famous local naturalist, is frequently shot by picture enthusiasts. On the north shore of the reservoir, the tracks of the Ulster and Delaware Railroad, moved at such great expense in 1913, now rust with disuse. A local group of entrepreneurs attempts to resurrect a portion of the line for use by sightseers.

As the reservoir has blended into the landscape, the trees planted in its infancy now mature, its shoreline cleared by the crews of Joseph Rice looking as if it had been washed clean by tides ebbing and flowing since the Ice Age, interest in the Ashokan Reservoir has shifted, in part, to concern over its recreational possibilities. Although the boarding house industry of pre-reservoir days has passed, increasingly, more and more city-dwellers come to the area to escape from the pressures of urban life and to refresh and re-create themselves. One can see as many out-of-state license plates as local ones on cars parked at the favorite fishing spots along its shore. For fishing in the deep, cold waters of the Ashokan, high in oxygen content, is consistently good, especially in the spring. As well as the promise of sport, the beauty and charm of Ashokan continue to draw people from the cities to the south.

Schoolchildren often ask about the cities they believe are hidden beneath Ashokan's waters, as if they had their own local legend of a mountain Atlantis in mind. They never fail to ask about the church steeple which some friend has heard someone else has seen rising from the depths like the Loch Ness monster. The old Stone Road in the East Basin, looking something like an ancient Roman way, surfaces from time to time in periods of drought, such as the summer of 1985, as do abandoned foundations and bluestone quarries. This road, usually submerged, went from the stone quarries in Morgan Hill and West Hurley to the train station in Olive Branch. The 18 inch wide, 4 to 5 foot long slabs of bluestone laid end to end are incised with deep grooves cut to hold the iron wheels of the heavily-loaded bluestone wagons. Near this road are also the markings of the last glacier. These glacial striations look as if some giant mountain lion had raked its paws across the once soft, wet rock. Some locals even believe that the Ashokan has changed the weather. One person states that it rains more now than in the past. Another, that a downdraft over the reservoir divides thunderstorms, splitting them up, and sending one part north and the other south.

Be this as it may, Ashokan remains a place of interest and even fascination. Yet, the resulting attention has been the cause of conflict at times. While the early patrolling and stringent inspection of the entire Ashokan watershed has been relaxed somewhat since the introduction of chemical purification processes, visitors and locals alike, at times, find themselves at odds with the City of New York and its representatives in Ashokan. Although the City does provide a number of jobs for local individuals, hired for the maintenance of the waterworks, most people who observe and use the reservoir, under special permit and with a current New York State fishing license in their possession, do not obtain income from the City, and thus are not always responsive to, or even knowledgeable of the City's local suzerainty and its strict enforcement. Those who innocently leave their cars and walk below the dam, or collect driftwood along the shore are frequently arrested and fined heavily for these seemingly innocent transgressions. In this regard, some local inhabitants consider the Board of Water Supply Police, the descendent of the police corps established during the era of construction, an occupying force. Others see the prohibition of hunting on reservoir property as unnecessary, especially during deer season, when many beleagured animals take refuge there. As a result, poaching is not uncommon, and feelings between the City and the town are not always amicable. Local officials, also complain about the poor maintenance of roads and bridges, and the haphazard plowing of the snow in the winter. The Traver Hollow bridge, found in the 1970s to be unsafe, was summarily and indefinitely closed by the City to the great surprise and inconvenience of the inhabitants of West Shokan. This state of affairs remained unremedied, the City alternating between threats of bankruptcy and promises of action, until the local State Assemblyman, Maurice Hinchey, took the matter in hand. This situation was reminiscent of a similar transportation problem which occurred in 1913, after the Shokan bridge had been toppled by high water and not replaced by the City.

Taxes, their amount and prompt payment, have also been a longstanding point of contention between the City and the local townships. Since before the dam was completed, when the City condemned and purchased the land, New York has believed that it has been treated unfairly by local tax assessors. It has considered these property taxes too high, and named them the "revenge of the locals."[92] This preception has resulted in a concerted and continual campaign by the City to initiate legislation to exempt municipal water systems from taxation. This effort began in 1910 with the introduction to the state legislature of the McKenzie bill, known locally as the "tax-dodging bill," or as A. T. Clearwater put it, the bill which violates a solemn agreement with the county.[93] Although this bill, which surfaced repeatedly for many years containing various new provisions, was never passed, it generated a condition of bad faith and mutual suspicion, which has lasted to this day. As recently as 1976, then Mayor Beame, faced with municipal bankruptcy, publicly considered the three possibilities of legislative exemption, renegotiation of taxes, and even default.[94]

In addition to this sense of distrust, many inhabitants of Ashokan feel that the City has not outgrown its original assumption that rural areas exist for the sole purpose of servicing growing urban centers. This position was first made emphatically clear in 1905 by City Corporation Counsel Delaney, when he conducted the first hearings in Kingston, and little change in this point of view seems to have occurred since then. In a recent article published in a prominent New York City newspaper, the name "Ashokan Reservoir" was misspelled, and its location placed incorrectly. Yet, although the article advocated the metering of water in the City in a time of great municipal wastage, it seems unlikely that this politically unpopular suggestion will be acted upon, much less enforced. For it would seem that New Yorkers believe that an unlimited supply of water is somehow their right by law. As if to reflect this assumption, in the City, presently, water bills are assessed on the basis of building frontage rather than usage. In 1978, at a public forum of the Catskill Center for Conservation and Development held in West Shokan on the shores of the reservoir, then Commissioner Francis X. McArdle of the City Environmental Protection Agency made his position specific on City water metering. It was unnecessary, he stated, and there would be none. And so, the "urban prejudice," as it is often called, continues to influence the City's public policy toward the rural area which provides its water. In this regard, the question might now be asked: although the City owns the land upon which the reservoir rests, who, if any one, owns the water? Possibly, this question can never be answered, at least not to the mutual satisfaction of all concerned parties.

In the 1970s, however, a move was made on the part of a local state legislator to introduce some type of "regional concept," as it was called, to provide for a greater measure of local determination in the matter of the use of the abundant waters of the Catskills. It was suggested by then State Assemblyman H. Clark Bell of the local 101st Assembly District, that a regional corporation be established to administer the operation of all municipally owned reservoirs. In discussing this bill, Bell called for an end to New York's "dictatorial control," and asserted that the City must be required to meter its own water usage. 240 million gallons per day would be saved, he anticipated, if this were done.[95] Although there was general agreement on the part of Ashokan inhabitants regarding these two points, questions were raised concerning the great cost of Bell's plan, the matter of the payment of taxes, and the likelihood that this large new corporation would simply substitute state for city control, and thus, once again, override the interests of the local people. Regarding Assemblyman Bell's additional proposal to open the Ashokan Reservoir to wider recreational use, such as swimming and motorboating, there was a mixed reaction. A few, with an eye for profit, felt that they might benefit financially from this proposal. Others, however, in the majority, asked serious questions. Would this Southeastern New York Water Plan and the expanded recreational use of the Ashokan Reservoir place an unmanageable burden on local services, and would the consequent increased second-home development drastically change the peaceful, rural, local lifestyle, making the area decidedly urban-oriented, its economy increasingly metropolitan-centered? Would not the area lose its integrity, its identity? By April 1975, however, the bill which had proposed and initiated the initial study of the water supply in the 13 southeastern New York counties expired, and the Temporary State Commission, which it had created to undertake this research, was disbanded, its work left incomplete.

And so, the debate over the Ashokan Reservoir and the proper and equitable use of its waters continues. What the future will bring, in this regard, no one knows for certain. However, it can be ventured, that although the shadow of unrestricted and unrestrained development in the area does fall on the road ahead, with New York City firmly holding the reins at present, the near distance seems safe. For it is unlikely that the City will willingly relinquish its control to another outside authority. And in this way, the City inadvertently acts to preserve both open space and the rural quality of the area. It also seems likely that the matters of maintenance of roads and bridges, the patrolling of City lands for trespass, and the payment of taxes will remain problematic, debated for generations to come. There is no reason to believe that a pattern of communication established more than a 1/2 century ago will change its shape overnight. Nonetheless, whatever the outcome of this continuing discussion, the Ashokan Reservoir remains, certainly, one of the most beautiful locales in New York State. It functions not only as a source of one of man's most precious necessities, pure fresh water, but also as a setting for tranquil recreation. Whatever our difficulties with discharging the most enlightened stewardship of this valuable resource, or exorcising the memory of what was given up and lost here in the childhood of this century, it would seem that, from the perspective of time, it is fortunate, all things considered, that the Ashokan Reservoir was constructed.

Footnotes

[1]Lazarus White, *The Catskill Water Supply of New York City* (New York: John Wiley, 1913), p. 15.

[2]White, p. 15.

[3]Alf Evers, "The Ashokan Reservoir is Built," T*he Catskills: From Wilderness to Woodstock* (New York: Doubleday, 1972), p. 591.

[4]White, p. 16.

[5]John R. Freeman, *Report Upon New York's Water Supply With Particular Reference to the Need of Procuring Additional Sources and Their Probable Cost With Works Constructed Under Municipal Ownership* (made to Comptroller Bird S. Coler), March 23, 1900.

[6]William H. Burr, Rudolph Hering, and John R. Freeman, *Report of the Commission on Additional Water Supply for the City of New York* (New York: Martin Brown, 1904).

[7]*Compilation of Legislation in Regard to the Water Supply of the City of New York* (New York: Board of Water Supply of the City of New York, 3rd edition, 1911).

[8]The Board was organized into bureaus which carried out its chief functions, the head of each bureau reporting directly to the Commissioners. There was the Administrative Bureau, headed by the secretary, which was in charge of accounting and recordkeeping and the purchasing of supplies. The Real Estate Bureau was charged with the acquisition of property by direct purchase and the adjustment and payment of temporary rentals and taxes on property acquired. The acquisition of most of the great areas of land required by the project by condemnation proceedings was given by law to the Supreme Court through the appointment of commissioners of appraisal. The

Police Bureau patrolled the labor camps of the contractors, protecting the local inhabitants from harm. The Bureau of Claims collected facts and kept records relating to claims for indirect damage to real estate not taken by the Board, but affected by its operations, such as damages to established businesses and also claims for loss of employment. The largest bureau was that of Engineering, with the Chief Engineer at its head. At the height of the construction, this bureau employed over 1,300 people. It undertook to make surveys and prepare maps, plans, designs, estimates, contracts and reports. It selected, inspected, and tested supplies, equipment and materials, and it supervised the construction and the upkeep and operation of the works. The great variety and extent of this bureau's functions, of course, necessitated a complex and well-administered organization. The bureau was divided into departments, divisions, and sections. There were a Headquarters Department and various field departments. Each department had four to six divisions, which were assigned work amounting to approximately 30 million dollars. There were Northern, Southern, and City Aqueduct Departments, the Long Island Department, and the Reservoir Department, which had charge of all work on the watersheds in the Catskills and at the headworks of the Catskill Aqueduct.

[9]Robert Ridgway, *Robert Ridgway* (New York: privately printed, 1940), p. 193.

[10]Ridgway, p. 162.

[11]Quoted in *Dictionary of American Biography*, 9 (New York: Scribners, 1964), p. 308.

[12]Charles Weidner, *Water for the City* (New Brunswick, New Jersey: Rutgers University, 1974), p. 181.

[13]Weidner, p. 181.

[14]Elwyn Davis, interview, West Shokan, New York, September 13, 1973.

[15]*New York World*, December 3, 1905.

[16]*The New York Times*, September 16, 1906.

[17]*Pine Hill Sentinel*, March 4, 1905.

[18]Kingston *Daily Freeman*, December 18, 1905.

[19]Also appearing were William D. Brinnier for the Ulster County Board of Supervisors; John G. Van Etten for the Eastern Dynamite Company; Frances A. Winslow for the City of Yonkers; and George R. Wood for Dutchess County.

[20]Elwyn Davis, interview, West Shokan, New York, January 19, 1974.

[21]Weidner, p. 179.

[22]Ridgway, pp. 164-165.

[23]A. T. Clearwater, letter to Thaddeus Merriman, February 17, 1931.

[24]*Pine Hill Sentinel*, December 2, 1905.

[25]*Annual Reports of the Board of Water Supply, City of New York*, December 31, 1906, p. 215.

[26]*Pine Hill Sentinel*, April 14, 1906.

[27]White, p. 77. See also Charles P. Berkey, *Geology of the New York City (Catskill) Aqueduct*, 146, No. 489, Albany, New York, February 15, 1911.

[28]*New York World*, February 21, 1906.

[29]Weidner, pp. 194-195.

[30]*Compilation of Legislation in Regard to the Water Supply of the City of New York*, Laws of 1905, Section 29, Chapter 724.

[31]Randolph Winston, letter of March 16, 1974.

[32]Winston.

[33]Mrs. Sam Ware, interview, Kingston, New York, May 31, 1974.

[34]Mr. Hutton, in Randolph Winston, letter of March 16, 1974. Under separate contract, James O. Winston also supervised the erection of the aeration plant, purification facilities, and the relocation of the Ulster and Delaware Railroad.

[35]*Annual Report of the Board of Water Supply, City of New York*, December 31, 1908, pp. 79-81.

[36]*Engineering News-Record*, August 5, 1909.

[37]*Pine Hill Sentinel*, December 12, 1908.

[38]"Housing Conditions and Wages on the New York State Barge Canal and on the Ashokan Dam, Board of Water Supply, New York City," *Engineering News*, 62, No. 6, August 5, 1909, p. 157.

[39]In 1910 1% of the population owned 47% of the property and received 15% of the gross national product.

[40]*Engineering News*, August 5, 1909.

[41]The president of the "Ashokan Bank," which also sold steamship tickets, was J. D. Lecky.

[42]There were a "Camp School," a kindergarten, and a night school staffed by four teachers, teaching in 1909 about 130 pupils: 47 American whites and the rest black or foreign-born, most of whom were Italian.

[43]C. S. Bergner, "Construction Camp Life: Ashokan Reservoir," *New York State Tradition*, Summer, 1970, p. 9.

[44]Davis, interview, February 22, 1974.

[45]Davis, February 28, 1974.

[46]According to Frederic Snyder of Kingston, New York, prejudice was also exhibited by a member of an earlier and successful immigrant group toward other newcomers, when during the work, an Orthodox Russian fell into a drainage canal, and the foreman, who disliked the struggling man thinking he was Jewish, looked down angrily at the poor man and said, "Youse killed the only man who could walk on water, now get out by yourself."

[47]Sergeants Carmody and Ocker, "The Catskill Reign of Terror," *Ulster County Townsman*, September 28, October 5, and October 12, 1967.

[48]These law enforcement officers were detached in 24 precincts along the Aqueduct from Brown's Station at Ashokan southward toward New York City.

[49]Frederic Snyder, interview, Kingston, New York, January 25, 1974.

[50]Stephen A. Abbey, *Ulster Square Dealer*, November 30, 1907.

[51]Brian Inglis, *A History of Medicine*, (Cleveland: World, 1965), chapters 9-10.

[52]Jennie Kerr, interview, West Shokan, New York, August 15, 1977.

[53]Davis, January 24, 1975.

[54]E. G. Nimsgern, *Illustrated and Descriptive Account of the Main Dam and Dikes of the Ashokan Reservoir* (Brown Station, New York, 1909), p. 9.

[55]*Catskill Water System News*, May 20, 1912, pp. 89-90; June 5, 1912, pp. 94-96. Also, *Annual Reports of the Board of Water Supply, City of New York*, 1910, pp. 97-98; 1911, pp. 99-100.

[56]Davis, January 19, 1974.

[57]*Catskill Water System News*, June 15, 1912, p. 94.

[58]*Catskill Water System News*, June 15, 1912, pp. 95-96.

[59]Kathryn L. Heavey, letter of March 25, 1974.

[60]Harold Harris, "A Story of Ashokan," *Treasure Tales of the Shawangunks and the Catskills* (Ellenville, New York: privately printed, 1955), pp. 119-121.

[61]Mrs. Hugh Kelly, interview, Olivebridge, New York, May 2, 1975.

[62]*Catskill Water System News*, November 20, 1913, pp. 247-248.

[63]Harlowe McClain, interviews, Brodhead and West Shokan, New York, January 15 and 25, 1974.

[64]Hobart Rowe, interview, West Hurley, New York, February 6, 1974.

[65]Evers, p. 592.

[66]*Pine Hill Sentinel*, December 12, 1908.

[67]*New York American*, September 16, 1907.

[68]*Catskill Water System News*, November 20, 1912, p. 139.

[69]Kingston *Daily Freeman*, May 23, 1910.

[70]In 1907, Cornelius Ver Muhle had appraised the entire reservoir site for land speculators at 34 million dollars.

[71]Weidner, p. 226.

[72]Kingston *Daily Freeman*, March 24, 1909.

[73]Davis, February 28, 1974.

[74]Weidner, p. 251. See also the Laws of 1905, Section 42, Chapter 724 in *Compilation*.

[75]Weidner, p. 238.

[76]Kingston *Daily Freeman*, November 27, 1907.

[77]*Annual Reports*, 1913, p. 21.

[78]Cited in *Cases of Commission No. 10, Ulster County General Business Damage Commission 2*, manuscript notebook, September 26, 1911-December 13, 1913.

[79]*Cases of Commission No. 10.*

[80]*Cases of Commission No. 10.*

[81]*Cases of Commission No. 10.*

[82]Kingston *Daily Freeman*, May 20, 1913, p. 5.

[83]Kingston *Daily Freeman*, May 20, 1913, p. 5.

[84]Kingston *Daily Freeman*, August 27, 1913, p. 10.

[85]Weidner, p. 264.

[86]Quoted in T. Morris Longstreth, "The Happy Valley," *The Catskills* (New York: Century, 1918), pp. 275 f.

[87]Mrs. William Burger, letter of January 27, 1974.

[88]Mrs. Ferris Davis, interview, Kingston, New York, May 31, 1974.

[89]Elwyn Davis, September 13, 1973.

[90]Elwyn Davis, September 13, 1973.

[91]Bergner, p. 11.

[92]*Catskill Water System News*, February 20, 1913.

[93]Kingston *Daily Freeman*, March 17, 1915.

[94]*Woodstock Times*, January 22, 1976. See also, November 13, 1975.

[95]*Woodstock Times*, August 8, 1974.

Selected Bibliography

Annual Reports of the Board of Water Supply, City of New York. 1906-1917.

"A. T. Clearwater," in *New York State Men.* Albany, New York: The Albany Argus Press, 1928.

Beers, F. W. *County Atlas of Ulster New York.* New York: Walker and Jewett, 1875.

Bergner, C. S. "Construction Camp Life: Ashokan Reservoir," *New York State Tradition*, Summer, 1970, pp. 7-11.

Berkey, Charles P. *Geology of the New York City (Catskill) Aqueduct.* Vol. 146, No. 489, Albany, New York, February 15, 1911.

Blake, Nelson M. *Water for Cities: A History of the Urban Water Supply Problem in the United States.* Syracuse, New York: Syracuse University, 1956.

"Brodhead's and Ashokan Reservoir," *Olde Ulster*, Vol. 9, No. 4, April, 1913, pp. 104-107.

Burr, William H., Rudolph Hering, and John R. Freeman. *Report of the Commission on Additional Water Supply for the City of New York.* New York: Martin Brown, 1904.

The Catskills, An Illustrated Hand-Book and Souvenir. Kingston, New York: Ferris Publication Company, 1897.

Catskill Water Supply: A General Description and Brief History. New York: Board of Water Supply of the City of New York, October, 1917.

Clearwater, Alphonso T. The History of Ulster County New York. Kingston, New York, 1907.

Commemorative Biographical Record of Ulster County, New York. Chicago: J. H. Beers, 1896.

Commissioner of Appraisal Proceedings. Found in the Division of Real Estate, Department of Water Resources, Municipal Building, Room 2417, New York City.

Compilation of Legislation in Regard to the Water Supply of the City of New York. New York: Board of Water Supply of the City of New York, 3rd ed., 1911.

DeLisser, R. Lionel. *Picturesque Ulster*. Kingston, New York, 1896-1905.

Evers, Alf. "The Ashokan Reservoir is Built," *The Catskills: From Wilderness to Woodstock*. New York: Doubleday, 1972.

Flinn, Alfred Douglas. "Dams for the Catskill Water Works," *Harvard Engineering Journal*, November, 1909.

Flinn, Alfred Douglas. "The World's Greatest Aqueduct," *Century Monthly*, Vol. 78, No. 5, September, 1905, pp. 707-721.

Fowler, Barnett. "Ashokan Reservoir," *The Conservationist*, June-July, 1948, pp. 14-15.

Fowler, Barnett. "Water for Gotham: The Reservoirs of New York City—built, building, and to be built," *The Conservationist*, August-September, 1948, pp. 14-15.

Freeman, John R. *Report Upon New York's Water Supply With Particular Reference to the Need of Procuring Additional Sources and Their Probable Cost With Works Constructed Under Municipal Ownership*. (Made to Comptroller Bird S. Coler), March 23, 1900.

Gill, Brendan. "The Gathered Waters," *The New Yorker*, December 31, 1949.

Hall, Edward H. *Catskill Aqueduct and Earlier Water Supplies of the City of New York*. New York: The Mayor's Catskill Aqueduct Celebration Committee, 1917.

Haring, H. A. *Our Catskill Mountains*. New York: Putnam, 1931.

Hasbrouck, Kenneth, ed. *The History of Ulster County with Emphasis upon the Last 100 Years 1883-1983*. Ulster County Historians, 1894.

Heacox, Cecil E. "Liquid Assets," *The Conservationist*, June-July, 1950, pp. 2-9.

"Housing Conditions and Wages on the New York State Barge Canal and on the Ashokan Dam, Board of Water Supply, New York City," *Engineering News*, Vol. 62, No. 6, August 5, 1909, pp. 154-157.

Inglis, William. "Submerging Eight Villages in a Drinking Fountain," *Harper's Weekly*, January 11, 1908, pp. 10-13; 32.

Kunz, George F. *The Mayor's Catskill Aqueduct Celebration Committee*. New York: Catskill Aqueduct Celebration Publications, 1917.

Longstreth, T. Morris. "Mount Ashokan and the Reservoir," *The Catskills*. New York: Century, 1918.

Merchants' Association of New York, An Inquiry into the Condition Relating to the Water Supply of the City of New York. New York, 1900.

Merritt, Edward Lawrence. *Cases of Commission No. 10, Ulster County General Business Damage Commission 2*. Three manuscript notebooks, September 26, 1911-December 13, 1913.

McClellan, George B. *The Gentlemen and the Tiger: The Autobiography of George B. McClellan, Jr.*, ed. Harold C. Syrett. New York: New-York Historical Society, 1956.

New York City Board of Water Supply, Catskill Water Supply: A General Description and Brief History. October, 1917.

New York City Board of Water Supply, Esopus Division, Songs. High Falls, New York, 1911.

New York City Board of Water Supply, Origin and Achievements of the Board of Water Supply of the City of New York. September, 1950.

New York State Historical Association Proceedings of the 13th Annual Meeting, Volume 11, 1912.

Nimsgern, E. G. *Illustrated and Descriptive Account of the Main Dam and Dikes of the Ashokan Reservoir*. Brown Station, New York, 1909.

Nineteenth Annual Report, 1914, of the American Scenic and Historic Preservation Society. Albany, New York, March 24, 1914.

Ramapo Improvement Company. *Proposal to the Sinking Fund Commission for a Supplementary Supply of Water for the City of New York*. New York, 1884.

Ridgway, Robert. "Department Engineer of the Board of Water Supply," *Robert Ridgway*. New York: privately printed, 1940.

Ruedeman, Rudolf. "Development of Drainage of Catskills," *American Journal of Science*, Vol. 23, No. 136, April, 1932, 337- 349.

Sylvester, Nathaniel Bartlett. *History of Ulster County, New York*. Philadelphia: Everts and Peck, 1880.

Temporary State Commission on the Water Supply Needs of Southeastern New York. *Alternatives: A Re-Evaluation*. Albany, New York, November 15, 1974.

Thomas, J. T. *Report No. 2 on a Water Supply for New York and Other Cities of the Hudson Valley*. New York, 1884.

Ward, Richard F. "Catskills' Treasury of Water," *The Conservationist*, June-July, 1960, pp. 2-4.

The Water Supply of the City of New York. New York: Board of Water Supply of the City of New York, September, 1950.

Wegman, Edward. *Design and Construction of Dams*. 8th ed. New York: John Wiley, 1927.

Wegman, Edward. *The Water Supply of the City of New York*, 1658- 1895. New York: John Wiley, 1896.

Weidner, Charles H. *Water for the City*. New Brunswick, New Jersey: Rutgers University, 1974.

White, Lazarus. *The Catskill Water Supply of New York City*. New York: John Wiley, 1913.

Zimm, Louise H. "Tongore (Olive Bridge) Gravestones," in manuscript, 1948.

Zimm, Louise H. "Water Supply," Southeastern New York, in Vol. 1, *New York*, 1946.

Index

About the Author

Bob Steuding teaches Humanities at Ulster County Community College in Stone Ridge, New York. He is also a State University of New York Faculty Exchange Scholar, and serves as the Poet Laureate of Ulster County. Among his books are two volumes of poetry, *Ashokan* and *Winter Sun*, a critical biography of the Pulitzer Prize poet Gary Snyder, and *A Catskill Mountain Journal*. Presently, he is at work on a new book, *Rondout: The Story of a Hudson River Port*, to be published by Purple Mountain Press.

Purple Mountain Press is a publishing company committed to producing the best original books of regional interest as well as bringing back into print significant older works. Recent titles have included: *Catskill Mountain Drawings* by Richard McDaniel and *In the Catskill Mountains: A Personal Approach to Nature* by Walter F. Meade. For a complete list write: Purple Mountain Press, Ltd., PO Box E-3, Fleischmanns, NY 12430 or call: 1-800-325-2665.